To Frank

with warmest ~~~ ~~~

John Hogg

22. III 69.

IMPELLED INTO EXPERIENCES

IMPELLED INTO EXPERIENCES

THE STORY OF THE
OUTWARD BOUND SCHOOLS

J. M. HOGAN

EDUCATIONAL PRODUCTIONS LTD
WAKEFIELD, YORKSHIRE

FIRST EDITION 1968

Published by

E.P. Publishing Company Limited

for

EDUCATIONAL PRODUCTIONS LIMITED

17, Denbigh Street, London, S.W.1.

© Educational Productions Limited and J. M. Hogan 1968.

Printed in Great Britain by Examiner Printers, Huddersfield

7158 0390 5

PREFACE

SIR ALEC CLEGG

When those who are now approaching retiring age were born, physical education in the grammar schools, which were the only secondary schools we had, was the responsibility of the drill sergeant or the retired professional cricketer, neither of whom had a place in the school staff room. It was a para-military activity concerned with muscle-building, with body as opposed to mind, with records, with the XI or the XV, and with competitive athletics, all carried on in a gentleman v. player context, and the inept were ignored.

To-day secondary schools of all kinds are adding climbing, sailing, caving, canoeing, ski-ing, underwater swimming and other activities to their games, athletics and gymnastics. A number of education authorities have established their own adventure schools and are taking the Duke of Edinburgh's Award in their stride.

How has this come about? There is no doubt that the main impulse was generated by the Outward Bound Schools established by the genius of Kurt Hahn, the former Headmaster of Gordonstoun. Exactly how this happened and how it all began might never have been recorded had not Jim Hogan, who established the first Outward Bound School at Aberdovey, not written this book. What he has given us is an important piece of educational history, described at first-hand with an ebullience which makes every page fascinating reading.

There are critics of Outward Bound who see it merely as a toughening process, but it is obvious from this account that its main operators, Hogan, Price, Lagoe and Fuller, have not seen it in this light, and this book should do much to dispel this impression. Indeed, those concerned with the development of education since the last war will immediately realise how Hahn's philosophy, revealed in the "duty to impel people into experience," is the same as that of the Hadow Report on the Primary School, which thought of education in terms of activity and experience, and also that of the Plowden Committee, whose conviction was that educationally "finding out is better than being told."

The whole education service has much to learn from these developments and there is great hope that we may at long last have escaped from the practices of talent spotting, training the strong and ignoring the weak, and cultivating failure by praising the adept and ignoring the inept. If this in fact does happen, the debt of education to the Outward Bound idea will indeed be great.

But the Outward Bound idea will, of course, change, as all sound education changes, according to the demands of a changing society. It should have no difficulty in doing this as long as it continues to be run by educators sensitive to the needs of youngsters and free to respond to them.

FOREWORD

by

SIR SPENCER SUMMERS, M.P.

Chairman of the Management Committee of the Outward Bound Trust since 1947.

It is something of a paradox that the founder and the pioneer of Outward Bound were both educators — Kurt Hahn and Jim Hogan — and yet the response to their work and to the subsequent promotional activities of the Trust, which was formed in 1946, was much more forthcoming from Industry than it was from Education — the reverse, incidentally, of the experience in Germany.

The professional educator tended then to regard the time required for an Outward Bound Course as provided at the expense of the time otherwise allotted for the acquisition of knowledge, or preparation for an examination. The claims of Outward Bound, whether of time, or aim, were seen in conflict with, rather than part of the true purpose of education.

The business executive or personnel manager, on the other hand, had no difficulty in recognising that the development of self-confidence, self-help, and self-discipline, brought about by an Outward Bound Course, reinforced and extended in a way not otherwise available the scope of industrial training. Moreover, it was primarily to Industry that we looked for the capital needed to develop from the original school at Aberdovey, of which Jim Hogan was the first Warden, to the present six Schools in this country offering training facilities, staff and advice to fifteen similar Schools abroad.

Most of those who have given so unsparingly of their time and talent, through service on one or other of the Committees or Boards of Directors that have been developed over the years, have contributed from a great diversity of experience. But few would claim a background of education extending beyond their school or university days.

In these circumstances, it is legitimate to wonder how it has come about that Outward Bound has become accepted as part of education, has attracted scholarships from Local Education

7

and has been permitted to maintain the pension rights of teachers who work in Outward Bound.

A large part of the answer is to be found, if not in the narrative of this book, at least between the lines. For to Jim Hogan, more than to anyone else, should be attributed the success inherent in this transformation. He it was whose fundamental thinking and penetrating analysis of what we were doing, or claimed we were doing, with his lucid and virile powers of expression, made sure that we never lost sight of the original purpose of Outward Bound — to contribute to the development of 'the whole man.' Hahn has described the task of the educator as "to transmit into manhood the attributes of childhood." The 'release' experienced, albeit subconsciously, by so many during an Outward Bound Course is part of that transmission. To that process, too, Jim Hogan has made a major contribution.

He would be the first to agree that Outward Bound is still developing, and breaking fresh ground, but in putting on record our history to date as he sees it, all who wish well to Outward Bound are more in his debt than ever.

Thank you, Jim.

CHAPTER 1

Today, if I were to be rung up late at night and invited to breakfast seventy miles away and then offered a new job about which I'd had no forewarning whatsoever by an almost complete stranger, I should regard the whole proceeding with the gravest suspicion. But today I am a local government officer and therefore insulated against any such possibilities. Twenty-seven years ago I was a young schoolmaster and, fortunately, my defensive mechanisms were scarcely developed at all.

Rejection from National Service on grounds of defective eyesight had left me with a compulsive obligation to justify my existence. There was plenty to be done in the schools, which were limping along with staffs that were often horribly depleted, as well as in a variety of organisations attempting to help the young whose home life was about to be violently disrupted.

Among those who came to replace the young men fast disappearing from the common room of my school was a devoted schoolmaster whose service had previously been in private prep schools. It was not long before I had inveigled George Blanchard into the out-of-school activities which then formed the major part of my interest. As our friendship grew he made constant reference to the similarity between the views I had formed and those which had long been held by Kurt Hahn, headmaster of Gordonstoun. I had not previously heard of Hahn and was impressed by what Blanchard told me. In reading reprints of Hahn's speeches I was captivated by the vivid formulation of principles towards which my own experience had led me to grope. When Blanchard planned to visit Gordonstoun and suggested that I should join him I welcomed the opportunity.

At that time the school had been evacuated from its former home near Elgin in Morayshire and was accommodated in Plas Dinam, the country residence of Lord Davies, roughly half-way between Newtown and Llanidloes in Montgomeryshire. On the journey there Blanchard gave me a brief account of the background of this remarkable man, Kurt Hahn.

The son of a wealthy German industrial family, Hahn had spent some time at Oxford where he had formed lasting friendships with many Englishmen. While still a young man he suffered a sun-stroke which was to leave him with a permanent disability over which he triumphed with the greatest courage.

His early career was in German politics and at the end of the First World War as secretary to Prince Max of Baden he became involved in the affairs of a country faced with the consequences of defeat. Prince Max's interests turned to education as a means of assuring the moral rehabilitation of his nation; as a consequence Hahn found himself in 1918 acting as Headmaster of a school at Salem on Lake Constance. He modelled the school on what he felt to be important in the English public schools in which many of his friends had been educated. Salem had achieved an international reputation before Hitler came to power and Hahn had declared himself as an open enemy of the Nazis. His condemnation of the Brownshirt murders led to his imprisonment and here his story might well have ended had it not been for intervention by English friends.

Hahn was released and allowed to come to England. Before long the necessary funds had been raised privately to provide the successor to Salem at Gordonstoun. I shall not refer at great length to the features of Gordonstoun practice and belief which distinguished it from existing public schools; there will be others intimately acquainted with the school who will wish to give detailed accounts of all that Hahn accomplished there. I must content myself with reference to a limited aspect of Gordonstoun achievement.

It was clear that Hahn's prime interest was in the kind of men his school would produce rather than in strictly academic accomplishment. He made great efforts to introduce his boys to the activities of the community immediately outside the school and particularly of those engaged in fishing and boatbuilding. Hahn did great service to education by emphasising the importance of experience of this kind. He was fortunate in his situation on the shores of the Moray Firth since seamanship was to become one of the highly developed activities of the school. The boys had the opportunity to handle small craft and side by side with this went the discipline of manning a coastguard service for that part of the coast. The school had been presented with a staunch fore-and-aft schooner, an ex-Bremen pilot cutter with auxiliary motors which was re-named the Prince Louis. In this craft crews of boys experienced the rigours of life under sail in the North Sea.

At Salem Hahn had dealt with many children whose health

and physique had been damaged by the inadequacies of war-time diet. He evolved a scheme of physical activity centred largely upon the basic athletic skills of running, jumping, and throwing. A 'training break' was set aside each morning when all pupils were encouraged to reach a set of standards. In due course Hahn sent Salem pupils to compete in the English Public Schools Sports at the White City. There they did themselves great credit, which is not surprising in view of the small amount of training for athletics which was undertaken in this country at that time, particularly in field events.

Hahn believed that a regular training break coupled with the goal of simple standards of performance (varied according to age) had advantages not only as a means to physical fitness but also in the general development of character. Each child was required to aspire towards all-round physical accomplishment. In Gordonstoun boys were expected to attempt to reach set standards in each of five sections — swimming, sprinting, jumping, throwing, and distance running or walking. A range of choice in each section was intended to meet the objection that some youngsters, by reason of abnormalities of build, would find success in certain activities permanently beyond their powers; in addition there were two levels of attainment — " Standard," which should be reached by normal boys but only after moderate effort and perseverance; and " Silver," which would remain as a goal for those to whom success might come too easily if they were to be confronted by average requirements. Although there was a choice within each of the four sections, success in at least one activity in each section was imperative. By this means, Hahn claimed, a boy was attracted into training because of his progress in those sections which he found most within his powers; ultimately he was confronted with the necessity of overcoming such weaknesses as had been revealed.

Hahn believed that fitness gained by regular athletic training of this kind would stand a boy in good stead in any situation demanding physical stamina and staying power. Those who led the boys on land expeditions into the arduous stretches of the Cairngorms, however, found that there was no necessary correlation between performance on the school tracks and jumping pits and the irksome plod through bad weather on the heights. Nor was perseverance in the face of physical obstacles any guarantee of patience in tasks of craftsmanship, study or skill.

Eventually Hahn evolved a three-fold challenge for his boys.

A scheme of qualification for a badge was set out. To earn the award boys had to pass the athletic tests as well as a simple test in swimming and life saving; they had to follow a voluntary interest known as a " project " to a predetermined stage of attainment, and complete an expedition on land or water. They had also to undertake to abstain from smoking and alcohol throughout their training and carry out conscientiously such training exercises as were prescribed for them.

Hahn arranged that the badge should be made available to boys from the neighbourhood, who were invited to make use of the school's training facilities. It finally became known as the " Moray Badge " and it was not long before Hahn was advocating the adoption of the scheme on a far wider scale. He was convinced that nothing could do more to stimulate training for fitness among the young than the establishment of a scheme of " County Badges " throughout the country; letters advocating such a scheme had been appearing in *The Times* and other papers sporadically for some years.

This was the sort of background information I received as Blanchard prepared me for arrival at Plas Dinam. There was much with which I found myself in sympathy. The concept of an " all-round " demand, for instance, had already seemed to me to be of real educational significance. It was with the greatest eagerness that I looked forward to meeting a man who had worked out the whole idea to an advanced stage and practised it apparently in dramatic and spectacular ways.

At the school I was put into the care of Henry Brereton, Director of Studies at Gordonstoun and an old friend of George Blanchard. Brereton told me much about the regime; about the differing colours of school uniform and the system whereby boys were given assignments of work and trusted to complete them or admit their deficiencies. He explained the important roles of the " guardian," or head boy, and the " helpers," or prefects, who had a real responsibility for the general conduct of the school. We wandered into the grounds to see the boys at athletic practice. They moved in groups from the javelin throwing area to the jumping pits, and so on. The whole thing seemed to take place in a quiet and leisurely way, supervised mainly by the boys themselves.

Suddenly I became conscious of an astonishing intrusion on the scene. A tall, stooping figure swept in long strides across the lawns. Although the morning was warm and sunny he was clad in a long black overcoat with astrakhan collar and a grey Homburg hat of positively Stetson dimensions. This was pulled down firmly on to his ears and tilted so as to cover the back of his neck. I learned the reason for this later but at the time I found difficulty in believing that the man who wrote in such passionate terms of adventurous pursuits on the sea and in the mountains could really present to the English countryside such a totally inappropriate front.

Blanchard introduced me to Hahn as though my views on education might be of some importance. He described in exaggerated terms the things I had done and expressed the conviction that I might have something to contribute to the County Badge campaign. My embarrassment was not reduced by the impression I formed that Hahn was not really taking it all in. He had a distant look in his eyes and punctuated Blanchard's panegyric with an occasional, slightly guttural, " Wonderful." The inflection, coupled with the air of being elsewhere, made it clear that Hahn was not impressed, nor could I blame him.

He turned on his heel to leave us as abruptly as he had come and I had no reason to feel that he had really become aware of my existence. Certainly I did not suspect that a meeting had taken place which was to change my whole career.

CHAPTER 2

Before leaving Gordonstoun we had a further meeting with Hahn. This time, we were indoors and it was clear that, despite his "protective" clothing, Hahn had found the bright sunlight outside extremely trying. As time passed I came to realise that his earlier sun-stroke had left him extraordinarily sensitive to excessive heat or light.

We learned more of what Hahn was trying to do in his efforts to spread the benefits of the Moray Badge type of training. Before leaving Scotland he had made considerable progress. The King George V. Foundation had made a grant of £2,000 in order to provide a cinder track on which training could take place in all seasons. Hahn had been approaching various trusts in the hope of establishing a training centre to be closely associated with the school in which boys from industry could enjoy for a short time all the advantages of boarding and make such progress as might lead them to continue their training elsewhere. Having failed to bring this about in Scotland, Hahn was renewing his efforts and hoped to develop on these lines in Wales.

A Committee had been formed to press for experiment with the Moray Badge idea, varied to suit the differing circumstances of other parts of the country. This Committee, known as the County Badge Experimental Committee, included distinguished educationists and people of influence in other fields. Little progress was being made because of the heavy demands already being made on such able-bodied men and women as had not already been called to H.M. Forces and, because many of the more orthodox workers in education and the established youth organisations were suspicious of Hahn's ideas.

Shortly after this visit the opportunity came for me to play a small part in the affair. There had been occasional outbursts of correspondence in *The Times* about the County Badge idea for several years and at this time a senior member of the hierarchy of the Boy Scouts Association contributed to the series and pointed out that there was little in the County Badge programme which could not very well be achieved within the context of the Scout movement. As a Scout Commissioner myself I was acquainted with the writer and wrote to him privately, sending a copy to

Hahn merely for his general interest. My argument was that while those who followed Scout training at least to the standard of the First Class badge would derive great benefit, the majority of Scouts did not in fact do this. In my view the failure to lead Scouts generally along a progressively exacting course of training was the principal reason for the unfortunate lapse of membership at or shortly after the age of fourteen. It seemed to me to be regrettable that Hahn should be discouraged from trying to do what Scouting was too commonly failing to do. Furthermore, the vast majority of young people were untouched by the Scout movement and I could see no good reason for denying them the possibility of being approached through other channels. This letter was to have a surprising consequence.

Some weeks later I was called from my class at school to take a private telephone call. It was Hahn speaking from Wales.

"Can you come to see me tomorrow?" he asked. I pointed out that schoolmasters did not absent themselves frivolously from their duties.

"But it is most important," Hahn assured me. "I cannot explain on the telephone but I wish to consult you urgently."

My repeated objection that I could not possibly ask for leave of absence except for the most convincing of reasons left Hahn totally unmoved.

"Who would you ask if you had such reasons?" he asked.

"The Director of Education," I said.

"I'll ring you back in twenty minutes," he replied.

What was said to my Director I do not know but within a very short time Hahn was back on the line telling me the time of the train from Wolverhampton to Shrewsbury. There, I was told, I should be met by a taxi to travel the remaining forty miles to Plas Dinam.

On the following day I arrived at Plas Dinam in the mid-morning and was shown straight to Hahn's study. This was a large, panelled and impressively furnished room which provided ample space for the sweeping diagonal marches he undertook when he became excited. Hahn asked me a number of questions about the kind of training I had been carrying out, none of which seemed to me of deep significance. Shortly he sat down and started to chew his handkerchief; then he drifted smoothly into sleep. I crept quietly from the room and set out on a tour of inspection.

15

By lunchtime the search for me was widespread and I was returned to the presence of my host, who was obviously mildly puzzled at my behaviour. We chatted over the meal and then I pointed out the need for me to catch an afternoon train from the nearby station of Caersws if I were to spare him the expense of a second long journey by taxi. Hahn was outraged. Of course I would stay the night. I explained that at 8.45 a.m. the following day I would be expected to be on duty in Wolverhampton and that my Headmaster would be concerned if I failed to present myself. Hahn had foreseen all this. On the following morning it was his intention to catch an exceedingly early train from Shrewsbury to London, passing through Wolverhampton. I would travel in his taxi and we should have the chance of further conversation.

At an unspeakable hour the following day I was roused and took up station at the main door as arranged. My driver of the previous day announced that, as usual, Mr. Hahn would be late and that, as we should certainly miss the train, the journey was entirely pointless. The longer we waited for Hahn the more he elaborated the theme. When Hahn finally arrived with his Bursar, Percival Pott, a flood of protest was met with, "Nonsense, my dear fellow; you always say that. There's plenty of time."

At intervals on that miserable journey through the wintry dark the lugubrious driver repeated, "We may just as well go back, Mr. Hahn. We're wasting our time thinking we can catch the train." It was all in vain. Hahn remained unmoved.

As we approached the outskirts of Shrewsbury Hahn proceeded to organise the transition from road to rail. Pott was instructed to repair at great speed to the booking office while Hahn and I tried to obtain seats. As we pulled up at the station, Hahn leapt ahead and up the steps to the departure platform. We heard the guard's whistle and hope drained out of me. As we ran on to the platform we saw the guard actually waving his flag. It must have been a novel experience for him to be pounced on from behind and have his arm abruptly snatched down.

"Not yet, my dear sir, my Bursar is still getting the tickets."

There ensued an argument during which acrimony on one side was matched by calm on the other. On sight of Pott however and recognising that the day was won Hahn took a leap at the carriage door which I was holding wide open. Unfortunately a misjudgment landed him full length and violently on the corridor floor. We went to the breakfast car in dusty triumph.

My next meeting with Hahn was equally odd. Early in 1941 I was struggling hard to preserve a youth club I had been asked to form in the middle of a large housing estate on the outskirts of Wolverhampton. Although few bombs fell in Wolverhampton itself, nearby Birmingham was suffering badly and it was impossible to be unaffected by the nightly "alerts" and the din of anti-aircraft fire. If one was guided solely by prudence and sent the club to the shelters each time there was an alert the whole thing was bound to fail. Thus one came to take risks—and to endure all the tension of acute anxiety. After one such evening I reached home at about 11 p.m. to be told by my wife that Hahn had phoned repeatedly throughout the day and had insisted that I should ring him on my return, however late that might be.

When Hahn came on the line I was astounded at his request.

"My dear fellow, can you take breakfast with me in the morning?"

"But of course not."

"But why? I assure you it's most important."

"Because Plas Dinam is seventy miles from here and I simply cannot get there."

"But, my dear chap, you have a car."

It seemed unnecessary to point out that petrol was then severely rationed. Hahn insisted it was imperative that I should go; as before, the reason was not one he cared to give over the telephone! The objection that my tank was practically empty and that all garages would be shut was pooh-poohed as trivial—the sort of difficulty that men of enterprise took in their stride. The current regulations for headlamps permitted two semi-circular apertures of only two inches diameter. Though one could manage well enough on familiar urban roads with their own dim street lighting, the prospect of a long run on strange roads (from which of course all signposts had been removed) was one I found daunting in the extreme. I said I would see what I could do. It happened that I had carried out sufficient Civil Defence duties in my car to have accumulated a small balance of petrol owing to me. It was just possible that I could obtain this from the post to which I was attached for part-time duty. To my secret chagrin I succeeded. There was therefore no reason, apart from acute fatigue and the warning of all my instincts, why I should not set out on my travels. I arrived at Plas Dinam at 5 a.m., completely exhausted, to be met by some unfortunate people who had been instructed to wait up for me. Once in bed I fell into a stupor but was shortly shaken into consciousness for the breakfast which I recalled was the prime object of my mission. Round the table were some impressive people, of whom, I am ashamed to say, I can at this date identify only one. This was Dr. A. D. (later Lord) Lindsay, Master of Balliol, who was the Chairman of the committee which had been set up to develop the County Badge idea. During breakfast Hahn struggled hard to bring me from my coma into the general conversation about the campaign. It is impossible that I can have contributed anything but evidence that I had undergone a trying experience. Very shortly the party disbanded and Hahn returned from the courtesies of farewell rubbing his hands with satisfaction.

"Splendid," he said, "They entirely agree with me."

"You must tell me what it is that elicits such community of view," I replied.

"But of course, my dear fellow. They agree about you—that you're just the person to become the Secretary of the County Badge Committee."

I came out of my coma! This was a design for which I was totally unprepared. Hahn soon explained why the moment was ripe for action. A sum of £300 was available, the gift of an anonymous well-wisher, he said. (I have since formed a shrewd view of where that money came from but I have no proof.) A pamphlet was all ready for printing which would put forward the whole scheme in a thoroughly convincing way. Approaches had been made to a number of trusts and Hahn had no doubt that once the pamphlet had been issued events would move irresistibly.

Exciting as the prospect seemed, I could not help but have misgivings. I was a married man with a young child. If I took such minimum of salary as would be essential and we were to bear the costs of publication, not to speak of travelling extensively to follow all reasonable prospects, the sum of money available was unlikely to last for more than three months at most. There was no guarantee that there would be more to follow. I concluded that the best thing I could do would be to seek secondment from my employers for a period of three months. If all went ill, I should not then have burned my boats.

I returned to Wolverhampton and presented a request for three months' secondment to my Director, Mr. T. A. Warren, a formidable man. Faced with a dwindling teaching force, he could not have been expected to welcome the idea. Patiently he explained the difficulties and hinted that association with people so obviously unorthodox would not be likely to commend me to the more stable members of my profession. Nevertheless he agreed to put the matter to his Committee but held out little hope of a favourable decision. In the meantime I discussed the matter with my wife, friends and colleagues. All came to a head when one of them pointed out the consequences this might have upon my pension prospects. At the age of thirty-three I was outraged that my actions should be governed by such a consideration and declared that if there was difficulty about my secondment I should feel obliged to resign. I was seconded.

CHAPTER 3

When at the beginning of June 1941, I took up the post of Secretary to the County Badge Experimental Committee I was fortunate in that Dr. Lindsay had arranged for me to have rooms in Balliol as my headquarters. This gave the advantages not only of a convenient base but also of close association with him while I learnt my way about in a totally unfamiliar field. It was extraordinary that one so much in demand because of his widespread interests could always find time to discuss other people's problems. He proved a fount of practical wisdom, kindness and encouragement.

On taking stock of the tasks to be accomplished it seemed that these divided themselves broadly under three headings.

First, and most urgent, we had to obtain the draft of the pamphlet, the publication of which was to launch a new drive for development and financial support.

Secondly, visits must be paid to people who were already experimenting with County Badge training, not only with the idea of offering advice where it might be needed but also in order that reference might be made to any success that was being achieved outside the special environment of a boarding school.

Thirdly, steps had to be taken to bring the Experimental Committee into full function. It had met formally on only one occasion. I learned from the minute book that in the previous month the Committee had authorised the opening of a bank account with the contribution of £300 from an anonymous donor. Those present included Dr. Lindsay, in the Chair, Dr. J. H. Oldham, Editor of the *Christian News Letter,* Mr. M. L. Jacks, Director of the Department of Education of Oxford University, Wing Commander J. G. Paterson, formerly of the Industrial Welfare Society but then Acting Director of Air Force Welfare at the Air Ministry, Mr. W. F. Oakeshott, High Master of St. Paul's School, Mr. W. Mc G. Eagar, of the National Association of Boys' Clubs, and Mr. H. Percival Pott, Bursar of Gordonstoun, serving the Committee as Honorary Secretary. It was obviously desirable that I should make the acquaintance of all these members of the Committee as well as of those who had not yet attended a meeting but had declared their willingness to serve. These included Professor (later Sir) Fred Clarke of London University, Mr. R. (later Lord) Birley, then Headmaster of Chaterhouse, Mr. Henry Brooke, M.P., Dr. (later Sir) Julian Huxley, Major General Sir Neill Malcolm and Sir Walter Moberley, Chairman of the University Grants Committee.

I travelled extensively, talking to educational groups and courses and visiting schools where County Badge work was in progress. At that time there were two experiments which seemed sufficiently well established to justify the hope that something significant might be learnt from them. The first was at Derby School, evacuated to a former camp school building in Hope Valley. It was there that I met E. G. Simm, the master principally responsible for this work. Though the work there was most encouraging the former day school had now become a boarding school and anything achieved there might be described as irrelevant to the general problem. For this reason I was most anxious to visit Hertfordshire. Here alone, at that time, a Local Education Authority had adopted the scheme experimentally and was prepared to award badges with the full weight and prestige of a large county. Training was taking place in day schools and, to a limited extent, in organisations catering for young people actually at work.

The impetus to development in Hertfordshire had undoubtedly sprung from the Chief Education Officer, Mr. (now Sir) John Newsom and his deputy, Jack Longland. What is more, they had introduced a new section into the requirement for the badge. It will be recalled that the original Gordonstoun system had consisted of physical tests based on a German Sports Badge to which the idea of dual standards of attainment had been added together with an expedition test. The final refinement in Scotland had been the addition of a "project" section which required patient application over a period of six months to a year to a task of study or skill. Hertfordshire had taken these three sections unamended and had added a fourth to be known as "Service." This had occasioned Hahn a great deal of misgiving. The giving of service was an accepted part of the natural order of living at Gordonstoun but he felt strongly that to make it a condition for an award of any kind was to court distortion of motives and was likely to lead to a debasement of the whole idea. Though I had some sympathy with this view, I was nevertheless conscious of the difference between the average school or club and life at

Gordonstoun with its Coastguard and Fire Services as well as the intricate pattern of activities contributing to the general development of the school. One could sympathise with those who felt that in less favourable circumstances it might be necessary to make quite specific demands for service to others. Thus the Hertfordshire idea of requiring positive training for competent service to one's fellows came to be accepted by the Experimental Committee and became the fourth section in the County Badge scheme as it finally emerged.

Towards the end of June I was acutely concerned that the draft pamphlet had still not arrived. A whole month of my three month's secondment had elapsed and we appeared further off than ever from the vital step that was needed to put our proposals in a form likely to commend them to the general public. Dr. Lindsay and Dr. Oldham, the two readily accessible members of the Committee, met me for a council of war. It was agreed that we should have to provide our own pamphlet and Dr. Oldham and I set ourselves to the task. As the experienced editor he was to polish the drafts and I was to supply the raw materials. Instead, as soon as we had roughed out our scheme we set ourselves a programme whereby we would each draft alternate chapters if possible daily. In fact we met to bring chapter drafts to final form three times in the first, and four times in the second week of July. By the beginning of the third week the final document was being duplicated for submission to the other members of the Committee and by the end of July we were hotly engaged in trying to assimilate the volume of comments and suggestions we had received.

My diary tells me that the proofs were cleared with the printers in the third week of August. The booklet came off the press in September—after my three months' secondment had expired and too late to assist us in raising funds for its extension. By then however much that was totally unforseeable had come to pass.

In the intervals between writing the pamphlet and articles for various educational journals, my visits to members of the Committee and potential users of the scheme had continued. It became obvious that guidance for leaders and teachers was imperative. The production of a comprehensive handbook of training could be regarded as a long-term measure. The most we could hope to accomplish in the immediate future was a concentrated training course for leaders, teachers and organisers. It was planned that this should take place at Plas Dinam during the last week in August. I conceived that this would be my personal swan song —since none of the financial support which Hahn had forecast showed any sign of materialising.

Plans for the leaders' course shaped well. We were lucky in being promised the services of two members of the Gordonstoun staff, both highly experienced in the athletics and expeditions training offered there. They were George (now Sir George) Trevelyan and Dr. B. Zimmermann. The latter was destined to play an exceedingly important part in our future activities. Like Hahn he had openly opposed the Nazis. He had represented Germany in international athletics and was one time German discus champion. Subsequently he became the head of physical training at Gutingen University where he introduced novel methods of training and achieved significant successes. His standing was such that he thought he could afford to dissociate himself from the Nazis, who were particularly anxious to engage him in their own training plans. Continued refusal so endangered him that he was advised to flee the country before he was arrested. Leaving all his possessions behind he walked out of his home to reach Switzerland and safety. There he received an invitation from Hahn to join him at Gordonstoun and continue the work for which he had such very great talents. "Zimm" spoke practically no English but so infectious were his enthusiasm and his humour that from the beginning no-one could resist him. When we met he had learnt a great deal of English but, entirely intentionally I am sure, he retained many quite extraordinary mispronunciations and introduced in the oddest ways strangely assorted English idiom so that most of his addresses and exhortations had a quality peculiarly their own. The overall effect was always the same. Wherever he was, there was merriment coupled with endeavour. Men and boys would do anything for him.

After handing in to the Oxford University Press the corrected proof of the County Badge booklet I travelled to Plas Dinam for what I thought would be the last week of my "secretarial" career. As soon as we had settled the programme of the leaders' course I discussed with Hahn my impending return to Wolverhampton. He took the view that it was unthinkable that I should forsake the cause now that things were beginning to move. It was in fact the last thing I wanted to do but I could not live without a salary— nor could my family. This seemed to me one of the simple facts of life about which people do not argue. Hahn did his best however. He suggested that I could very easily take up residence at Gordonstoun with my family until the tide had turned. By this time I had seen a good deal of Hahn's mode of life. About his pioneering spirit and educational perception there could be no doubt whatsoever—nor about his determination to see things through to the end. About his judgment in individual circumstances, however, I had come to have some reservations. On a number of occasions in the past few months we had had our differences. Frequently, no doubt, I had been completely in error but there had been occasions when events had proved me right. But opposing Hahn was a testing business. His exasperation could mount very quickly and when roused he would thunder at his critics, shaking his forefinger from his greatly superior height and flashing his eyes with righteous rage and indignation. I am bound to say that I always found this extremely wearing; it would have been easy to shrink from the conflict. Without at least the outward appearance of independence I think I should have found it impossible to keep Hahn within what seemed to be the bounds of the reasonably practical. Thus we were at an impasse. He thought me ungracious and prickly; I thought him unrealistic.

Typically, when we met the following day Hahn had an entirely different plan to propose. He had come to the conclusion that in spite of all our efforts the conversion of our critics and opponents was unlikely to be affected by preaching and persuasion. What we needed was a training centre in which we could put on a "compelling demonstration"—a place in which youngsters from industry could be given a "training holiday." I was the obvious choice for the Wardenship of such a centre; thus the whole problem of my security would be solved!

There was, of course, only one difficulty about this. If we saw no prospect in the immediate future of raising the funds to maintain a modest secretariat, it seemed unwise to visualise such an access of capital as would enable us to found an educational institution. Hahn explained that these were two entirely different things and revealed the details of a plan that had patently been growing in his mind over a long period of time.

When Gordonstoun moved from the Moray Firth to Plas Dinam, some thirty miles inland from Cardigan Bay, the loss of seamanship as a school activity had pained Hahn deeply. He had soon taken steps to have sent down by rail two cutters and a small dinghy. By hiring an underemployed boarding house at Aberdovey he had been able to arrange for parties of boys to undergo some small boat training. This however represented a pale shadow of their former activities. Without the sea-going schooner the whole enterprise lacked bite. In war-time, with most of our coastal waters restricted and hazardous, most people would have been happy to leave well alone. Hahn however had discovered that the Admiralty were prepared to permit sailing in a defined area of Cardigan Bay and he had therefore contrived to bring the Prince Louis also to Wales. I recalled the summer's day when he had visited me in Oxford, plagued by the heat and labouring under obvious strain while the schooner was making passage through the Caledonian Canal and down the West coast. All this had been made possible by Laurence Holt, a Liverpool shipowner, who had loaned the skilled men for the voyage. It was obvious that any further use of the vessel would be similarly dependent on the co-operation of someone of equal influence and stature. How far this was understood between them it was impossible to discover. It was true that Holt must have been greatly impressed by Hahn's work at Gordonstoun. He had subscribed the necessary funds to establish scholarships for boys from the local fishing community who might go from Gordonstoun to officer cadetships in his company; perhaps even more significant, he had sent his own son Julian to the school.

Besides being the senior member of the family business of Alfred Holt and Company, the owners of the Blue Funnel and other famous shipping lines, Laurence Holt was also a governor of the training ship Conway and there must undoubtedly have been discussion about the possibility of both schools contributing something of their respective traditions to a new venture. The schooner Prince Louis had anchored near the Conway on her passage to Wales and Hahn must have been conscious of the importance of securing the co-operation of a school which had an established reputation among seamen. Later I had good reason to believe that much thought must have been given to the launching of a new school at Aberdovey. At that time, however, I could extract nothing positive from Hahn. Preoccupied as we all were with the day-to-day conduct of a course for experienced people I was compelled to pay a flying visit to Aberdovey to see for myself the schooner and a house which Hahn believed to be available for purchase. To my inexperienced eye the ship represented no more than a promise of exciting possibilities. The house, though beautifully situated, would require careful investigation and considerable modification. Given reasonably ample funds there was a good chance of doing something enormously attractive. Hahn had no doubt that the requisite financial support would in due course be forthcoming. I had no reason to share his faith. Each day we lectured to the course and Zimmerman, Trevelyan and I walked the neighbouring country with the students. Each night, thoroughly tired, I faced Hahn's insistent argument that I should resign my job to launch the new training centre. Equally insistently I replied that all I needed was one solid piece of evidence that Laurence Holt or anyone else had made up his mind to provide the funds. Hahn became steadily angrier. Men of that kind, he said, could not be rushed precipitately into such undertakings. Men of my kind, I assured him, did not irresponsibly render themselves unemployed. The impasse continued.

On the Thursday night of this strenuous final week, at about ten p.m., Hahn capitulated.

"You are quite right, Hogan. We must put the matter to the issue. If you will go to see Laurence Holt and put the scheme to him I will phone him now."

It was useless to protest that there was no "scheme." Hahn's mind was made up and within minutes an appointment was being made for me to travel to Liverpool on the following day— the last day of our much neglected course.

In the mid-morning of the Friday I presented myself at the Holt residence in Liverpool—then being used as the head office of the firm—thoroughly frightened of the situation into which I had allowed myself to be rushed. Conscious as I was of the impertinence of approaching a distinguished businessman with a half-baked proposal hastily thrown together in the small hours it was too late for withdrawal.

Laurence Holt received me most kindly and introduced me to Brian Heathcote, who was adviser to Alfred Holt and Company on the recruitment and training of their staff. He was entirely in Holt's confidence and well informed on educational affairs. From then until lunchtime, some two hours later, I was questioned on the details of a proposal which could scarcely have been less carefully conceived and for which I could certainly not have been less well prepared. The guiding light lay in the appreciation one quickly formed about Laurence Holt's total dedication to the improvement of training for the sea. It was clear that he deeply regretted the passing of the square-rigged ships in which earlier generations of seamen had received their basic training. He believed that, denied engines and complex instruments, men had developed a sense of wind and weather, a reliance on their own resources—physical, nervous and technical—and an almost spiritual sense of fellowship and inter-dependence. The lack of these qualities seemed to him to be responsible for much of the loss of life by enemy action then taking place in the Battle of the Atlantic. He had studied the accounts by survivors of their ordeals in lifeboats and on rafts and was conscious that the majority of those going out to face similar hazards were completely unprepared for them.

It was not too difficult to envisage an amalgamation of our separate purposes. The County Badge plan could readily encompass the sort of preliminary training Holt required, the project embracing a knowledge of small boat handling and all the associated techniques, the expedition developing tenacity and initiative in strange situations. As for service—all the boys we were likely to receive were committed to hazarding their fortunes if not their lives for the future of the nation. The more we talked, the clearer it became that we should reach agreement upon what we could and should attempt to do. Little was said about the vital matter of resources and finally Holt left me with Heathcote to run briefly through the material requirements of money and skilled manpower.

At lunch we were joined by senior members of the shipping company. To my eyes they were all frighteningly crisp and businesslike. One was no longer dealing with idealists or theoreticians. Everything I said seemed impractical and unrealistic in this company. Hope dwindled.

Then, suddenly, Laurence Holt struck the table and made a short announcement. "We'll support you. We'll give you £1,000 outright. We'll buy the house and put it at your disposal and we'll lend you without charge the trained men you need for the nautical side of your training. How will that do you?"

Joy and dismay jostled in my mind. In almost every respect this was astonishingly good. But even I was aware that £1,000 would go a very little way towards furnishing and equipping a complete boarding school as well as financing its running costs until a steady income was assured. Nevertheless, what was one to do? This was plainly a moment with great dramatic quality and Laurence Holt was by no means unaware of this. To have niggled about one item might well have imperilled the whole. On the other hand, to pass it by might indicate sheer incompetence—a total unawareness of the facts of life. I looked at the faces around me to gather some clue as to their expectation. They were calm and impassive. It was a case of "do or die."

"Hahn will be delighted beyond measure," I said. "Now we can really begin to work out the details."

I envisaged a careful plan of campaign during which it would be possible to turn in other directions for the additional funds which undoubtedly would still be required. And with such a generous promise as a foundation, it ought to be possible to elicit further support. Holt's next words however shattered this illusion.

"How many can you take immediately?" he said.

"When we get into the house, without adaptation, twenty-four boys and resident staff," I said.

"Right. We'll send eight on each course from Conway, Gordonstoun should send eight and we'll provide eight more from this company until you can widen the recruitment. Let's say you'll start on October 4th."

"But," I gasped, "that's only five weeks from now."

"What's wrong with that?" asked Holt, rather coldly.

I explained that the owners of the house were living in it; that they would no doubt expect some time to obtain other accommodation even when they were sure of a sale; that an enormous amount of furniture and equipment had to be bought in the difficult war-time market; that staff had to be selected and engaged.

"Don't you want to start the school?" asked Holt.

"Indeed — but — "

"4th October it is," he said. "When we make up our minds we move. We expect you to do the same."

Throughout the return journey to Plas Dinam my mind wrestled with what seemed the insuperable problem that had been raised by this decision. I arrived as the course was in the middle of its farewell celebration and whispered my news and my misgivings to Hahn. Nothing could dismay or discomfort him however.

"Nonsense," he said to all my cautionary words. "We shall raise

28

more money. It cannot fail now."

He made a formal announcement of the day on which the new school would open and then proceeded to fix an appointment with my Director of Education in Wolverhampton for the next morning. I was due back at my job on the following Monday and we had to persuade him to accept my resignation forthwith. Even if he were to agree to waive the formality of notice the next five weeks would be busy enough. On the Saturday morning Hahn was in irresistible form. When we walked out of the Education Office in Wolverhampton I was free to apply myself to the impossible.

CHAPTER 4

The next month is memorable as one of incessant movement and frenzied activity. First there was a visit to London to meet potential directors of the limited company which was to be established for the management of the new school. One of these was reputed to be a financier of great experience and, I innocently assumed, vast resources. It was at least conceivable that he might represent some sort of insurance against the short term embarrassments that seemed quite inevitable. It was disheartening therefore that he concluded our first interview somewhat as follows:

"Be under no illusion, Hogan. I look to you to keep the whole thing under sensible financial control. Of course we're all behind it to a man. It's a thoroughly worthwhile affair but we must keep our feet on the ground. We all admire Hahn's educational vision and we don't mind putting our hands in our pockets for the odd fiver, or even tenner, you know. But we don't want any damn nonsense, understand."

For some time this injunction was to hang heavily on my consciousness; certainly it made me excessively apprehensive about spending even upon essentials.

Having seen the lawyers about the purchase and leasing of our future home in Aberdovey, my next call was in Oxford where final arrangements had to be made for the publication of the County Badge booklet. It was necessary, too, to settle my own future relationship with the Experimental Committee. At last there was some prospect of assistance from one of the educational trusts that had been approached. This made it possible for the Master of Balliol, as Chairman, to suggest that henceforward half of my salary should be paid by the Experimental Committee and half by the school; this would enable me to preserve freedom of action and to continue to spend some time working for the extension of the Badge scheme. These matters settled, the end of the week saw me back in Aberdovey arranging for the survey of the premises by the local architect, a charming person whose affection for the house was obvious from the first.

"Bryneithyn" was a solid residence on the north bank of the Dovey estuary some half a mile from the village. The road inland to Machynlleth followed the river and from it the drive swept up in a steep zigzag through beautifully timbered banks.

The house was of grey stone and all the main rooms faced due south. The view across the estuary made an instant appeal. The constantly changing banks revealed by each ebbing tide and the incessant variations of light and shade on the hills behind Aberystwyth gave it a quality which was to grow upon all who stayed there. Here was an asset which outweighed all the petty disadvantages we had yet to overcome.

"Bryneithyn" itself contained no more rooms than were to be expected in a generously planned family residence though many of them were perhaps more ample in scale than is common. Fortunately there were other buildings in the forty acres of grounds which constituted the estate. Potentially the most important was a commodious stable block with living quarters at first floor level. This offered an obvious possibility of conversion to dormitory space. There was also a useful cottage, known as the "Red House" and a small farm but both these were tenanted and unlikely to fall vacant in the near future.

The owner of the estate was living at Bryneithyn with her daughter. To them we owed a very great debt for the skill and care with which the grounds had been developed. The house itself was built on an extended terrace cut from solid rock. From the front the ground fell away steeply by way of a well planted rockery to a lower terrace on which was a pleasant lawn, flanked on both sides by mature wood. To the rear and on both sides of the house were skilfully planted outcrops of rock and further woodland with most attractive paths and glades. Bryneithyn itself was in a perfect suntrap as was a walled garden still higher on the hillside.

The architect agreed that by a comparatively simple operation we could bring the stable block into use as a sizeable dormitory with a minimum of toilet and lavatory space for night use. My major concern however was about the adequacy of the water supply and arrangements for sewage disposal. Enquiries revealed that the house drew its water from a spring which overflowed into a steep gully running behind the stables. I was assured that it had never yet caused any serious trouble. I elaborated on the differences between the consumption of a family of two with servants and a school intended to reach a total of sixty or seventy people.

We then turned our attention to the question of sewage. At that time all the household effluent flowed into a cess-pool situated in

31

the trees alongside the lower lawn. This was obviously very close to the rock and one was bound to be anxious about its capacity.

These two matters which were in the future to become a a source of embarrassment and inconvenience were blandly dismissed.

The architect was asked to plan for the immediate conversion of the stables—henceforward to be known as the "Bunkhouse"—and the provision of showers and washplaces in outbuildings behind the house. Tenders were to be invited from local builders in the hope that the essentials would be available as early as possible in the new year. This pre-supposed that my next dash— to the Office of Works at Cardiff—would yield the necessary building permits. Until the completion of this new work the number of trainees would have to be restricted to twenty-four.

The next problem to be resolved was that of furniture, equipment and supplies generally. This involved visits to the Board of Trade and Ministry of Works in London. Though the necessary permits were secured without grave difficulty, it was when one established contact with potential suppliers that the real obstacles became apparent. Most of the things we needed were simply not available for civilian purchase on the required scale. The only furniture suitable both to our requirements and our purse which proved to be readily obtainable consisted of wooden two-tier bunks of the kind used in civil defence as well as folding tables and benches of a particularly fragile construction. Bedding and most of the range of household equipment we sought were not to be obtained at all. The time seemed ripe for an S.O.S. to Alfred Holt and Company. Either they would have to come to our assistance or the starting date would simply have to be postponed. A telephone call resulted in an invitation to submit lists of all requirements which could not be met in the ordinary market. There seemed little doubt that all our needs could be furnished from the company's stores in Liverpool.

One other problem called for urgent solution—that of staffing the school. So far as sailing and seamanship were concerned we were entirely in the hands of Laurence Holt and could only trust that he would choose generously and well. The general supervision of shore-based training, however, required a competent schoolmaster. I would have to absent myself from the school from time to time in order to ensure recruitment for future courses as well as to carry out my commitment to the

County Badge Committee. It was therefore imperative that we should secure a first class house master. Hahn spoke confidently of a "Gordonstoun-trained housemaster" being provided for each of the 28 day courses we intended to run. This seemed to me to be unrealistic as a long-term arrangement and I feared the lack of continuity which it implied. However, the choice for the first course was admirable; Hahn was exultant when he informed me that the War Office had agreed to the secondment of Major F. R. G. Chew, a Gordonstoun housemaster in peace-time, who was then serving under Lord Rowallan at the Highland Fieldcraft Training Centre in Scotland. Though I had not previously met the man who was, in the course of time, to succeed Hahn as Headmaster of Gordonstoun, I had heard enough about him to realise that this was a piece of exceptional good fortune.

This was not the only drain on the Gordonstoun bank. I had realised that Zimmerman was the ideal partner in the job we were about to do but overtures to secure his translation were received with incredulity. All I could do, to begin with, was to arrange that he should come to us half-time. Step by step however, Zimm's involvement at Aberdovey increased and before long it was formally recognised that he belonged to us though would be available to Gordonstoun "for consultation" as required!

A further piece of robbery resulted in Miss Grace Hamilton, an assistant housekeeper at Gordonstoun, becoming the new house-keeper at Aberdovey.

One week before we were due to open most of the difficulties seemed to have been resolved. If all promises were kept we should be "operational" on the day.

On Monday, 29th September, I returned to Aberdovey to see if, in fact, everything was going according to plan. It was dis-couraging to discover that the family were still in residence at Bryneithyn. Their efforts to remove their possessions had run into the usual war-time difficulties and on Friday they left without their belongings.

On Saturday morning, a chief steward of the Blue Funnel line arrived to help us sort out our affairs. On the same train came the first batch of cadets from the Conway and from Liverpool. We arranged for them to eat lunch at a cafe in the village. They were then immediately pressed into an operation which must have taken them very much by surprise. They manhandled all the furniture from Bryneithyn into the Bunkhouse. As each room was emptied, scrubbing-out commenced.

In the meantime I was directing the transport of our goods from the station. An enormous consignment had accumulated there and it was not easy to ensure that the more vital requirements went off in the right order. It was arranged that as each room was cleaned at Bryneithyn the boys carried in our own furniture.

I soon became conscious of certain important deficiencies. We were aware already that the Aga cooker we had ordered had not been installed. We now knew that it had not even arrived. What was more, we appeared to be without any culinary equipment, crockery or cutlery of any kind. There was but one ray of hope. The Prince Louis lay at the wharf and a raid revealed an assortment of pots and pans, a collection of well chipped enamel plates and mugs, some nondescript knives, forks and dessert spoons and — a single teaspoon. Meanwhile my wife was drawing on her skill as a Cub-master and was constructing a camp kitchen in the open yard at the rear of the house.

When the final party arrived on the evening train, the battle had largely been won. Sleeping quarters for twelve boys and all the staff had been organised in Bryneithyn itself. Mattresses and bedding for the other twelve boys had been transported to the Prince Louis which would have to serve as a dormitory whenever she was not at sea until the Bunkhouse alterations were complete.

In due time the entire course sat down to a satisfying meal and duty squads washed up our limited equipment between courses. The establishment which had been publicised as " The Aberdovey Sailing School" had been brought into being, as Mr. Holt had insisted, on the 4th October 1941. This had been rendered possible by the contributions of a large number of people, including three women who had driven themselves without mercy, and were to continue to do so for a long time to come — my wife, Miss Hamilton, and Mrs. Katie Jones, a part-time maid recruited locally.

CHAPTER 5

We planned to run eleven courses a year, each of 28 days duration. This had seemed the longest period for which youngsters were likely to be released by their employers and at the same time the shortest in which we might give them a solid sense of achievement and progress. Though initially a large proportion were bound to be committed to careers at sea it was of the utmost importance that the effect of our training on non-seagoers should be put to the test. It was disturbing that Gordonstoun and Conway had both determined that their contingents should spend only one week at a time at Aberdovey. Initially, therefore, we were faced with eight boys from the Blue Funnel Line staying the full four weeks and sixteen from Conway and Gordonstoun changing over each Saturday. As events turned out, this may have been no bad thing at least for the first month. As a long term arrangement however, it seemed to me intolerable and something which had to be changed.

On the first Sunday of the course the boys were conducted round the neighbourhood. One of the most exciting prospects for them was the cruise on the Prince Louis and they were happy to spend some time examining her both above and below decks. She was moored alongside the large timber wharf which formed an important feature of Aberdovey's waterfront, relic of the days when a great deal of the merchandise for mid-Wales must have been off-loaded there. Immediately adjacent was a group of large timber sheds the majority of which had long fallen into disuse. The largest of these had been leased for our use and was to form the headquarters of all of our sailing activities. In command there was a Blue Funnel mate. The fact that his arm was in a sling and that he appeared to be crippled with pain from neuritis was no doubt, sheer bad luck but seemed no good augury for the small boat programme. Standing by for visitors, also, was Captain J.P. Williams who was to skipper the schooner. He confided at once that this was no port for a sailing ship with $11\frac{1}{2}$ feet of draught. He had consulted the local pilot and formed the considered view that we should start the school elsewhere. I broke the news that this was an idea that would not readily commend itself and moved the party on somewhat hurriedly. Experience over the years was to give strong support to the Captain's view. At that date, however, I was simply terrified at the suggestion that our whole project might have been founded on a fundamental miscalculation on a matter of such importance.

Back at the school we assembled the staff and discussed the plan of campaign. Chew joined us during the evening and I outlined my idea of dividing the boys into teams or, as we came to call them, "watches" of twelve, each with its own captain and vice-captain. It was clear that for some time we should have to call on the boys for physical labour rather than the training we had envisaged. Before they could carry out their daily period of athletics, for example, Zimmerman had to show them how to make their own jumping pits, run-ups, shot-putting circles and the like. Before boats could be sailed they had to be rigged and carefully overhauled. Nevertheless, by Sunday night we all knew each other and had our programme for the following days clearly defined and understood. On Monday morning we went into action.

My memories of the first course are fragmentary. It was not a time for the keeping of a diary. Every Friday night sixteen boys left us and sixteen reports had to be prepared after consultation with the staff. Every Saturday sixteen replacements arrived. Chew saw to the good ordering of affairs at Bryneithyn with calm assurance — Zimm went furiously about the preparation of facilities for his beloved athletics training. The nautical side of our venture was the one that needed a sense of direction and it fell to me in my lamentable ignorance to assess what was being done.

At the wharf there were conflicting demands. The schooner had been lying unattended for some months and needed a great deal of refurbishing. In daily attendance upon her were her bosun and her engineer. As soon as a party of boys appeared they were seized upon and harried into useful employment. On the wharf the temporary and disabled seamanship instructor had been joined by Ellis Williams, owner and operator of the Aberdovey/Borth ferry service which was virtually in abeyance for the duration of the war. Ellis was to become an invaluable sailing instructor but at first the officers were more concerned to get all the small craft seaworthy than to bring one or two into active service at once. No single element of the exciting programme we had planned was really in operation. My sympathies were with the boys.

The prospects of getting the schooner to sea were equally dismal. Captain Williams insisted on my meeting the Dovey pilot. It became clear that we should be acting most improperly if we allowed the Prince Louis to leave or enter the estuary unless he was in charge of navigation. As we had no small motor-craft to convey the pilot to and from the ship this threw up an obvious difficulty — as well as a source of additional expenditure.

Hahn had constantly insisted that it was my duty to understand all the factors affecting safety. Accordingly I was taken out to study the channel through which the ship would have to make her way to the open sea. This, as Captain Williams pointed out, was "like a dog's back leg." From her moorings the ship had to get into mid-stream as quickly as possible in order to clear a sand pit running out from the north shore immediately beyond the wharf. She had then to proceed to an inner buoy marking the beginning of a prolonged bank running out from the southern shore. Two further buoys indicated the channel of deeper water to the point at which, given a sufficient depth of tide, it was safe to cross "the bar."

The bar was to dominate a large part of our activity and it was some time before I came to understand something of its character. From my first introduction I merely gathered that it was a long tongue of sand stretching in a vast arc from the southern to the northern shore at the extreme "mouth" of the estuary. The river water scoured a fairly narrow channel, rarely more than about a hundred yards wide, but this shifted with some regularity. At one time it would be possible to sail a comparatively straight course almost due west from a point clear of the wharf and gain easy access to the waters of Cardigan Bay. The channel, however, then tended to shift steadily towards the north shore. This resulted in a more complicated course having to be steered to the actual crossing of the bar. Worse still, as the passage moved closer to the north shore it became necessary to sail for a longer distance parallel and, finally, dangerously close to the shallow northern shore itself. When the prevailing south-westerly winds were forcing the vessel towards this shore the situation was fraught with danger. Fortunately things rarely remained long in this state; the cycle was resumed as the channel silted up and the river forced through a fresh passage further to the south.

A further complication had to be explained to me. As a total landlubber I had always assumed that "spring tides" occurred only in the spring. I now learned that each month the tides alternated from their largest to their smallest variations. Thus at the maximum variation the tides flowed to a higher and ebbed to a lower point and were known as "spring tides." Correspondingly two weeks later, at the period of "neap tides," the difference between high and low water would be very much less. Captain Williams made it clear that the schooner would be unable to cross the bar at all during the neap tides since even at high water there would be insufficient depth over the bar for our deep keeled vessel. For about one week in four the schooner would be obliged to remain either in or out of her home port.

One thing seemed clear. As Aberdovey was then an almost untrafficked port no recent soundings had been taken and the buoys were well off position. This would have to be remedied forthwith. It seemed to me that if this were to be done by the staff of the school and if thereafter they were to traverse the passage with some regularity they should in time become very well qualified to navigate the ship in and out of the estuary without the assistance of a pilot who had obviously had no recent demands upon his skill. This proved an unpopular observation. Nevertheless, the arrangement to which we finally came left us entirely responsible for our own navigation.

For two and a half weeks of the first course Captain Williams continued his efforts to convince us that we should move the school elsewhere. Thus two sets of Gordonstoun and Conway boys had passed through the school without the schooner trip which they regarded as the highlight of the whole affair. Overwhelmed at last by the weight of opinion against him the Captain resolved to sail on an early afternoon tide. In tremendous excitement the Prince Louis left the wharf. I myself motored rapidly along the coast to a point at which one could see from above the distant passage over the bar. Undoubtedly there was a heavy sea there. For what seemed an age the gallant little ship plunged and tossed, apparently unable to beat the still flowing tide and the rollers coming in from the Irish Sea. I began to see the Captain's arguments as something more than an exhibition of debating skill. Perhaps he had been right all along. Perhaps the whole enterprise was reckless and ill-considered. My concern and anxiety mounted until at last it appeared she had broken free from the area of white water. It was true. She steadied and began to put on sail. Soon she was a picture heading out into the bay.

We had planned for the ship to be out for three days. It was disconcerting the following morning to be told she was cruising just outside the bar. According to intention she should have been well up in the north of the bay. In the early afternoon as soon as the tide had given sufficient water on the bar it was plain that she was coming in. I hastened to the wharf for an explanation.

"Never again: Not at any price," the Captain assured me. During the passage of the bar, which I had witnessed on the previous day, most of the boys had succumbed to sickness and a number from that time forward had taken a very limited interest in the proceedings. Course had been set for sheltered anchorages in the north of the bay. Long before reaching his objective, however, the Captain was overtaken by darkness and the southward set of the ebb tide. In war-time, of course, no lights were permitted on shore and through the long winter night the ship was kept under way while the Captain was uncertain of her position. As dawn broke, Captain Williams asserted, he found himself off Fishguard, which was well to the south of Aberdovey and protected against intruders by defensive minefields. It became still more difficult to reconcile Hahn's exhortations about safety with any suggestion that Captain Williams should be urged to hazard himself yet again. This was a time for consultation with the nautical experts in Liverpool and a conference was arranged. For the remainder of the first course we were reconciled to the idea of using the ship as a dormitory!

The Prince Louis' capacity for causing us anxiety was not yet exhausted however. The Captain now became concerned about her lying alongside the wharf. Although she had stayed there without damage for many months it was argued that we only needed spring tides and a southerly gale to pound her against the wharf and cause really serious damage. The idea therefore was to take her into mid-stream where she could lie safely at anchor. This meant that all who went aboard her had to be ferried across either in the ship's own small lifeboats or, whenever we had a crew available, in one of the school's cutters. At the time of spring tides this became a hazardous undertaking. I recall a boat load of adults trying to go aboard when a large tide was flowing powerfully up stream. Twice the rowers failed to beat the tide and we finished well above the ship. The third time the Captain took the tiller and steered us down river of the ship and then allowed us to drift back. It soon became clear even to a novice that we were being swept at a rapidly increasing rate directly on to the sharp bows of the vessel. This was suicidal. Protest soon became noisy. The Captain took in the situation and shared our alarm. Just in time he called on the oarsmen for a violent effort. We swept just clear of the bows and bumped and slithered the entire length of the ship quite unable to halt ourselves. I began to have the gravest doubts about my change of occupation.

An episode which caused us to bring the Prince Louis back to the wharf occurred on the day the boys were to leave for home. A number who were to travel on a later train remained on the ship to make all tidy. When it was time to take them off the wind and tide made it impossible for us to get a boat out to them and we were obliged to telegraph to their parents to explain their non-appearance. It all seemed to me a funny way to run a school.

One other episode remains in my mind from the first course. Because of the uncertainty about the qualification of the staff who might at anyone time be assembled at Aberdovey it seemed prudent to define fairly narrowly the activities in which we would try to excel. Hahn had very different ideas On the one hand, he thought we should reconcile Headmasters of schools and Principals of Technical Colleges to the loss of their youngsters for four weeks if we could inform them that some continuity of academic and technical study would be assured. My protests that a degree in history gave me a limited competence to instruct classicists, engineers and chemists were treated as evidence of a lack of enthusiasm and resource. On the other hand, Hahn wanted us to emulate Gordonstoun in the range of exciting interests that could be followed. We were all well aware of his enthusiasm for bloodhounds. From time to time a boy would be sent out to lay a trail and others would follow the hounds as they bayed their way in pursuit. Certainly this was a skilful device for giving point to a gruelling cross-country run. Nevertheless, I had seen the forbidding creatures in action and had built up what was no doubt a purely personal prejudice against them. My reaction therefore was speedy when Hahn, in an excess of magnanimity, offered to lend one of his favourite hounds. I explained that we had a wide range of commitments and anxieties and would prefer to postpone further development.

When the Gordonstoun contingent for the third week arrived I was horrified to see the boy Anderson — a notorious hound lover — detraining with Macbeth, a canine monster of unbelievable ugliness. All one could do was to make plans for the safe accommodation of the animal until he could be escorted on the return journey.

40

CHAPTER 6

By the time we had launched our second course a number of significant changes had been effected. First, Conway and Gordonstoun had agreed that their boys should stay with us for a full four weeks. Secondly, we had been joined by Tom Phillips, a Blue Funnel Line Chief Officer of great practical ability and physical toughness. Thirdly, there had been a steady build-up of the amenities. We no longer ate in squalor but had endeavoured to provide at Bryneithyn some contrast to the severe conditions with which the boys were confronted during a large part of their training. Zimm too had been making marked progress and boys were now able to practise the athletic skills instead of paving the way for others. We entered upon this second month with high hopes.

During the first week consideration of the future role of the schooner was in the forefront. Eventually, at an impressive conference, it was agreed that Captain Williams should sail on a late morning tide the following day. Mr. Holt seized the opportunity to bring a distinguished party to speed the ship on her way.

Immediately after casting off from the wharf instead of striking out for deep water in midstream the schooner was steered straight ahead and within a hundred yards she was hard aground where she was bound to remain till the time of the next high water at approaching midnight.

I expected Mr. Holt to be nonplussed by the outcome of his morale-raising expedition. On the contrary he declared himself delighted. As the vessel had deep fine lines she was in a position of real jeopardy. Had she been allowed to keel over as the tide ebbed she would have lain at such an angle that the next incoming tide would have filled her as she lay. It was imperative therefore to shore her up with heavy timbers before she began to lean. This presented Mr. Holt with a welcome practical exercise which had to be carried out with some sense of urgency.

The following morning the Prince Louis was on her way once more on what was to prove the first round trip to be completed according to plan.

It was at about this time that I learned of Laurence Holt's wish that we should be known henceforth as the "Outward Bound

Sea School." Though the title "Aberdovey Sailing School" left a great deal to be desired my response to the new suggestion was hostile. It seemed to me unfortunately reminiscent of Richard Vanes's play "Outward Bound," which was concerned with the reactions of a group of people recently deceased and on passage to the next life. I could not be expected to foresee that a day would come when the Outward Bound Schools would be much more widely known than Vanes's successful stage play.

Later in the second month the schooner gave us the greatest period of strain that we had yet undergone. The absence of shore lights made night cruising in the confined waters of Cardigan Bay unthinkable and the alternatives once the ship was out of port were to cruise out in the Irish Sea with all the dangers of collision on the convoy routes or to seek anchorage in the north of the bay. The most attractive course was to make for St. Tydwal's Bay close in to Abersoch. This gave shelter from all except east winds. In all but the worst conditions the ship's boats could go ashore which, in the event of her being weatherbound, offered a change of scene and a chance of replenishing stores.

Some distance along the north coast of Cardigan Bay was the small harbour of Pwllheli. This might have been ideal as an alternative port of call but the entrance was even more difficult than that at Aberdovey and could be undertaken by the Prince Louis only in conditions of calm and high water. Finally, if strong winds blew either from the north-east or east the only course open was to anchor as close in as was safe to Criccieth so as to take advantage of such shelter as the land afforded.

In November, 1941, the ship left Aberdovey with the remainder of the short winter daylight in which to make her anchorage. She hastened to St. Tydwal's and, because of the threat of wind, put down both her anchors. Unfortunately the wind blew up to gale force from the south-east, which put the ship in very great hazard. She was too close in and the weather was too severe for her to have any hope of sailing out. Her two petrol-paraffin auxiliary motors were useful for manoeuvring her to and from her moorings but were incapable of giving her headway against gale force winds and heavy seas. There was nothing she could do but ride out the gale and for us to pray that her anchors did not drag.

Shortly after the gale blew up the cable of the heavier of her two anchors broke so that the anchor and fifteen fathoms of cable were lost on the bottom. The safety of the ship and all on board now rested on a single anchor. Hour by hour throughout the days we 'phoned the coastguards at Abersoch. It was no use enquiring during the long hours of darkness since then no one could tell whether she was holding or dragging her position. I believe the Pwllheli lifeboat might have taken the boys off but it was a gamble as to whether there was less risk in trying to ride it out. In the event all went well and after eight days of unabated tension and anxiety we knew she was safe and returning home. The boys were dirty and drawn but quietly triumphant. It is hard to be sure whether they knew how near they had been to disaster.

The ship was fitted with new and heavier anchors and cables throughout and hours of post-mortems were held. I began to realise how great were the responsibilities we had undertaken. Hahn did his best to leave me in no doubt on this issue. All the time the ship had been in hazard he had badgered me with enquiries to a point where our exchanges became increasingly terse. The necessity to carry on the heavy duties of establishing the shore-based part of the training while bearing the anxiety about the movements of the ship was such that one could readily give way to impatience and irascibility. I was by then feeling the strain of the varied functions into which I had been driven. At Aberdovey responsibility for the general direction of training was coupled with all the detailed concerns that would normally fall to a busy bursar. To that had to be added the necessity to build up a publicity campaign so as to secure a widening of recruitment. In addition I was commanding the Gordonstoun unit of the A.T.C. which involved visiting there at least once a week. Finally, the publication of the County Badge booklet had stimulated a demand to address gatherings widely scattered throughout the country. During the second month I helped with a week-end conference for organisers and teachers in Hertfordshire, accompanied Hahn to an important meeting in Leeds and attended a meeting of the Experimental Committee in Oxford. There I was able to report that the first 2,000 copies of the booklet had been distributed and that a further 2,000 were being printed. The first responses to our application for financial support were now coming in and we soon had sufficient funds to ensure our continued activity for at least another year or so.

Rising interest in the idea of extending the badge scheme so that it might meet the needs of adolescent girls led to invitations being sent to women who were playing a leading part in youth work to join the Committee. As a result Miss P. Colson, Secretary of the Central Council of Recreative Physical Training, Miss E. V. Sparks, Youth Organiser for Hertfordshire, and Miss Honoria Harford, Secretary of the National Council of Girls' Clubs, all agreed to lend their help. It was obvious that we were on the threshold of a considerable advance but my personal capacity to force the pace and at the same time do justice to the needs of Aberdovey was open to serious question. While Chew was in control there one could leave with confidence but at the end of the second course he was to go and there was no certainty about his replacement. John Newsom, Chief Education Officer for Hertfordshire, was making it clear to Dr. Lindsay that the experiment there had advanced much more rapidly than could have been foreseen and that, if they were to avoid serious blunders, they felt they ought to be able to turn to the Experimental Committee for the loan of my services full-time at least for a period. This was, of course, out of the question. Yet acknowledged failure — either at Aberdovey or in Hertfordshire — would have been disastrous. It was against this background that I returned to Aberdovey to bring the second course through its concluding stages.

There was no doubt that real advances had been made. All of the boys had been to sea — some rather too long! All had made marked progress in athletics, in small boat sailing and in a variety of assignments in general seamanship graduated to take account of previous training. Only the expedition was still at a very elementary level — being little more than an arduous day's walk. Nevertheless enthusiasm had been stirred and in some cases the boys had distinguished themselves. It was with some feeling of satisfaction that we looked forward to the end of the course and a respite over the Christmas holidays. Our dismay can be imagined when during the last days it was discovered that there was an outbreak of mumps among the boys and that a considerable number had to remain until they were free from infection!

The spirit of goodwill during our Christmas break was further marred by the slow progress of the people who were carrying out the conversion urgently needed for our expansion. Staff and equipment were available to train at least 48 boys on each course and as long as we were obliged to limit our intake to 24 we were losing income.

At the wharf Tom Phillips was thinking out a series of improvements. An important addition for which he pressed was the setting up of a pair of ship's davits on the wharf itself. We had already experienced the need to bring up the heavy cutters for overhaul and repair and he had demonstrated his capacity to improvise with sheer legs and block and tackle. Nevertheless it was obvious that properly installed davits would enable us to lift even our heaviest boats from the water with very much more confidence. What is more if we were to acquire a full-sized ship's lifeboat it would be possible to practice lifeboat drill, which would obviously prove of the greatest possible value to those boys who were about to go to sea. And so another trickle of valuable equipment was opened up. In course of time the wharf shed was to become a well-packed store of marine equipment; spare oars, masts, spars, sails, ropes and line, lifejackets, signal flags, compass binnacle, charts, even disused small craft fully rigged. Few of the orders had been issued by me and there was no immediate sign of bills flowing in; nevertheless one could not escape apprehension about what would happen if they did!

Shortly after the meeting in Liverpool when Laurence Holt first committed himself I had received a letter telling me that £1,000 had been paid into an account *in my name* at the Midland Bank, Aberdovey. This was an astonishing act of trust but it also underlined my personal responsibility for the finances of the school. I was beset by anxiety, therefore, as expenses mounted and income remained pathetically low. All was to be well, however. Though, I believe, Alfred Holt's kept a record of the stores that were issued with such generosity, much of it became and remained a concealed subsidy for which we had the greatest reason to be grateful.

The delay in building up our numbers, however, brought us to a stage of real embarrassment. Often the payment of accounts had to be held up until fresh fees were received for advance bookings. Characteristically Alfred Holt's came to our rescue with a further cash gift and at the same time made our needs known to such other people as might be persuaded to help. One of the earliest responses came from the Mercantile Marine Services Association which committed itself to a contribution of £1,000 per annum. Thus we scraped through the initial difficulties.

CHAPTER 7

We had said "Goodbye" to Chew in December, 1941, with very real regret. He had come to us when we were in a state of chaos and exerted a reassuring influence throughout. In January, 1942, he was succeeded by Captain Farnell, another ex-Gordonstoun housemaster seconded from his regiment for two months. Much of the initial work of organisation was now complete and Farnell was able to devote more time to training activities. He, for example, first led boys on expeditions away from our nearer hills. Any who had illusions about their fitness would be hard put to to remain with Farnell when in gym shoes he dashed up and down Cader Idris as a sort of light-hearted romp. I saw less of him than I would have liked, however, because of a new and most distracting development.

Early in the new year the Master of Balliol warned me that John Newsom was pressing for me to be seconded to Hertfordshire to look at the general organisation of their County Badge scheme. Modest though the development had been it had nevertheless exceeded the capacity of the County staff who were responsible for its conduct and organisation. Unless their problems were solved Newsom threatened that the experiment would have to be abandoned. Alarmed as we all were at this prospect it was impossible to leave Aberdovey without a Warden. I suggested a compromise — that for the middle two weeks of every course for, say, three months I should work in Hertfordshire, thus enabling me to spend the first and last week of each four week course at Aberdovey.

This arrangement took effect in February and March in the middle of which Farnell completed his time with us. No further replacement could be obtained from H.M. Forces and during the middle fortnight of the March course the gap was filled by a master released from Gordonstoun for the single fortnight. There was no prospect of a successor to him. It was therefore against this background of stop-gap staffing at Aberdovey that I made my visits to Hertfordshire.

Educationally there was nothing dramatic about what I was able to do in Herts. A number of devoted and conscientious people were doing their best to apply a scheme they had learned about only from the printed word. What they needed was practical advice and constant encouragement. In February and March I did all that I could to fulfil this need but the price was heavy. In order to save working time I made all my journeys by night and at week-ends when the rail services to Wales were sparse indeed. The memory of the night hours spent waiting in unheated and unlighted compartments in lonely sidings still remains stark and vivid. Even more vivid, however, is the recollection of the pressure which could not possibly be maintained. The prospect that in April there would be no housemaster at all finally turned the scales. I reported as fully as I could on what I had seen and what seemed to be needed to put the experiment in Herts. on a sound footing. The most important recommendation was that a permanent organiser should be appointed. The report was accepted and as a result in due course E. G. Simm, who had done such good work at Derby School, took up the new appointment in Herts.

From April onwards I was able to concentrate on building up at Aberdovey. By this time the conversion of the bunkhouse was complete and we could accept first 36 and later 48 boys. Without a housemaster one was committed to 24-hour duty and it was at this time that we introduced a new feature. Previously all the staff concerned with the schooner and small boat sailing had lived either on board the ship or in lodgings in the village. From now on we insisted that those not permanently attached to the ship should live at Bryneithyn and undertake some of the duties of supervision. This was far from being popular and it was some time before junior officers were found to whom the responsibilities of "pastoral care" were in any way acceptable.

Our daily programme was now fairly well defined. The boys were called at 7 a.m. and immediately took part in a loosening run round the grounds, followed by 50 skips. They then went through the cold showers and, after dressing, tidied their dormitories. Breakfast at eight was followed by final cleaning of all the sleeping quarters, dining-room and grounds. Before morning prayers and flagbreak, which took place at 9 a.m., there was a full inspection and points were awarded to each watch for the standard of cleanliness and good order they had reached. After a simple ceremony of "colours" and prayers the watches set out according to the timetable to the daily round of activities.

One watch might spend the first half of the morning cleaning ship on the schooner, learning her ropes and how to handle her sail. At mid-morning they would change over with a second watch, and, according to the state of the tide or progress through the course, take out one of the cutters, under oars or sail, learning the part of each man in the boat. Each boy in turn took the helm and experienced alternately the thrill of sheering through the water and the cold panic following a misjudgment in our difficult tideway. After lunch the same watch might have a period with Zimm learning the tricks of putting the weight or competing against the stopwatch over 100 yards. Before tea there would be a period of bends and hitches, morse or semaphore signalling, rule of the road at sea or chart work. Between tea and dinner the period might be reserved for letter writing, and after dinner either a free evening or organised talks by a succession of people who had survived the hazards of war and had a tale to tell. At week-ends the programme was varied. If the weather was exceptionally favourable on Saturdays there might be voluntary sailing. Otherwise the afternoon and evening were free. On Sundays after morning church there were practice expeditions in the hills immediately to the north. It was a busy programme.

That the boys tackled their training with real zest was due I think to two simple devices. First of all we explained and observed the County Badge training programme. From the beginning each boy knew his personal target. The table of physical performances, according to age, was set out plainly on the notice board. A "project" or a programme of technical training was determined for each boy so as to take account of his previous experience. If he was a Conway Cadet the seamanship requirements would be very high indeed. The boy would be thoroughly tested in boat handling, signalling, navigation and so on. If he was completely new to nautical affairs a programme would be set which would present him with the necessity for hard work but which should not be beyond his powers.

The expedition section would be covered by the report of the Captain on the boy's performance at sea and by a one day hike during the final week-end of the course. Just as the nautical tests were graduated so as to take account of the boys' starting point so the expeditions were graduated so as to take account of the medical report on the state of fitness he had reached.

At first the array of demands was met with incredulity. When we spoke at the opening meeting of their ultimately walking over

30 miles across Welsh mountain country we were always conscious of politely subdued derision. Nevertheless as each course advanced what Hahn called "the magic of the puzzle" began to appear. Each boy had a personal record book and could take most of the tests at any time. Zimm, for instance, was adept at holding up all the proceedings whenever a boy jumped or sprinted or threw to the required level of performance. The result was ceremoniously entered in his book. As the course advanced even the least promising would see a splatter of entries in their books and the possibility of adding more began to appeal to them. By the third week in a course this really became a force to be reckoned with. It was not uncommon during off-duty periods to discover the most unlikely youngsters prowling up and down the grounds of the house mouthing the rules of the road at sea or the points of the compass while others lashed themselves around the jumping pits. We now had to reflect on the dangers of over-stimulation and counsel the virtues of restraint.

Similarly, in the expeditions there was good reason to proceed with caution. A salutary experience lives in my memory. One of the parties which had been given an exacting route was very late in returning. Long after dark I walked in the direction from which they were bound to come. The last mile or two was over main road but there was a point where the road swept in a broad curve and a rough track offered an obvious short cut. Halfway along the track I met the party which was in good spirits but one man short. I was assured that he was perfectly all right but had preferred to keep to the road. It appeared that he had had trouble with his boots which had raised painful blisters and that for the last few miles he had been walking in his socks! I hurriedly retraced my steps and set out along the road. Long before the boy came into sight I could hear him whistling apparently as cheerful as when he had set out. When he approached I flashed my torch to take in a sorry picture. His boots were slung by their laces around his neck; his socks were holed and blood-stained.

He rejected my offer of a lift and pleaded with me to allow him to continue. There was no doubt about the boy's sincerity and with the gravest misgivings I let him finish the job.

As well as the personal challenge of the badge requirements there was the additional spur of inter-patrol competition. Apart from general orderliness, we had linked a number of activities to the daily competition. The watches were responsible for proceeding under their own discipline from Bryneithyn to the Wharf which was about a mile away. Officers observed and reported on their bearing and punctuality. When boats were prepared for sailing the boys were responsible for seeing that all the gear was correctly assembled (including oars, sails, anchors, compass binnacles, bailer) and that every member was complete with lifejacket. Similarly at each point the punctual arrival of the watch with all the necessary training equipment was the subject of assessment by the officers.

Perhaps the most spectacular of the events in the daily inter-watch competitions was the lifeboat drill which was introduced in 1943. The first time a watch did this it would take several minutes to go through all the operations. We looked forward to the possibility that a well-trained watch might bring the final time down to about one minute. In due course we were to see performances below 50 seconds as by no means exceptional. It illustrated the capabilities of the young when once their interest is fully engaged.

The only reward for excellence was the honour of flying the watch pennant on the school flagstaff and it may seem extraordinary that young men in their late adolescence should be moved to such extremes of endeavour for so unsophisticated a reason. That of course is to over simplify what takes place. The delight of working with a well-trained team is a powerful force and we were to discover that it can manifest itself at least as powerfully in activities of this kind as on the sports field. In fact the activities which were patently related to the rescue services had an appeal entirely of their own as we were to discover later in quite different environments.

From the spring of 1942 until I left Aberdovey at the end of 1944, there was to be no startling change in the general pattern of things we did but rather a gradual striving to do them very much more effectively. In some ways this was made more difficult by a steady increase in recruitment of boys and of our capacity to accept them. It may therefore make for a clearer account if in the following chapters I concentrate in turn on the various aspects of development.

CHAPTER 8

Our capacity at Bryneithyn, including the Bunkhouse, was stretched to its limits with a course of 48, even though a watch of 12 boys would be aboard the schooner for a large part of the time. At first this was no serious handicap since it was difficult to recruit a full course, but it was soon clear that private applications were going to increase rapidly. We were compelled to turn down some who wished to come on the courses from July to September, which could be fitted into the school holidays. It was bitter to refuse the badly-needed income and for some months we accepted more boys by hiring a small marquee, but this was an unsatisfactory arrangement and we were constantly scheming to increase our permanent accommodation.

Before we could plan for large numbers we had to solve some problems. The first was the supply of domestic staff. Alfred Holt's had sent women stewards who in war time could not go to sea, but they could not endure the drudgery of kitchen chores and the boredom. Then it was suggested that we should accept as cooks and houseboys some of Holt's Chinese staff. They could not be compelled to go to sea during the war and so long as they could not be repatriated they had to be paid; it seemed sensible to take advantage of this.

Most of the Chinese were accustomed to a peculiar pidgin English which caused embarrassing misunderstandings. Some, however, spoke no English and understood little more. But to admit this apparently involved a "loss of face" which was to be avoided at all costs. One little cook continued to serve for breakfast what we had ordered for lunch and vice-versa, in spite of explicit and repeated instructions.

Although the Chinese were a tremendous boon they presented us with problems. Those from Shanghai and the Cantonese would not live in harmony and there were outbreaks of quarrelling. Later, when it became necessary to send one of the team back to base, all the Chinese set simultaneously about their packing. "One go, all go," they said. And so they did.

There were other problems. An official of the local council informed me that a complaint had been received about the discharge from our cesspool. As our numbers grew and the load increased, the shallow cesspool had become saturated and was leaking directly on to the main road below the house. It was necessary to empty the pool; inquiry revealed that when the job had been done in the past a bottle of whiskey had been supplied. We donned our Wellingtons, collected our shovels and containers, and set about the cesspool with vigour. No sooner had we penetrated the upper layers than I saw the point about the whiskey.

Funds had to be found for the re-organisation of our entire drainage system and the construction of an adequate septic tank. It was after my time that the school achieved the final improvement by installing a pump to force the effluent a quarter of a mile uphill into the main drains of Aberdovey.

We had similar difficulty over water. At first when our supply gave out we had to haul tanks of water from the wharf by means of a trailer. There was some difficulty about extending the public supply and we had to make do with improvised arrangements for many years.

Our accommodation was extended by a long series of developments — some carefully planned and others fortuitous. When the tenants of the Red Cottage withdrew we were able to fit it out as a pleasant sick bay with some rooms for officers. The next step was to add a hall on to the side of Bryneithyn and to link it to the kitchen at the rear. We were able to buy the lease of a neighbouring house, Braich-y-cellyn, which had been allowed to fall into decay. We decorated the house and stables with our own labour and materials and made it possible to accept over 100 boys. Then we obtained a pleasant house, Brynmeddyg, high above the village. To Brynmeddyg went my family and the school office; in addition we housed the Captains of the sea-going craft when they were ashore.

It had now become possible to accept 120 boys on each course. From this time, the role of the Warden was to change. In the early courses I had known every boy reasonably well and even when the numbers reached 60 it was possible for the Warden to establish a direct relationship with each boy. Now my role became increasingly administrative and the real task of education fell upon other shoulders. For me a great deal of the spice had gone out of the job.

CHAPTER 9

In some ways the least spectacular, the part of our work which came under Zimmermann's guidance was nevertheless of the greatest importance in the total task. Painstakingly he built up the facilities needed for athletics training. In this he derived very little advantage from our terrain. There was just room on the terraces below Bryneithyn for high and long jump pits and "run-ups," together with a shot-putting circle. For javelin and discus he had to take the boys to a neighbouring field in which it was just possible to contrive the necessary areas of comparatively level ground. Sprinting simply had to take place on the main road — fortunately at that time untroubled by any weight of motor transport. Even so, look-outs had to be posted if accident was to be avoided, and, if necessary, traffic had to be halted until a practice or test had been completed. We developed a technique for ignoring even the blackest of black looks!

For the two-mile run and the five-mile walk Zimm marked out appropriate stretches on the Abderdovey-Towyn road. As I toured other areas of the country and was told of the shortage of athletics facilities for County Badge training an account of our attack on the problem at Aberdovey always provoked the surprised disdain of the sophisticated. To appreciate the enthusiasm that was injected into the majority of boys one simply had to see Zimm at work with them. For those who tried there was never failing encouragement but for those who did not there was a richly varied commentary, the product of a salty and often vulgar humour. There were few indeed who resisted for long.

Very early in our history we found that the performances in the events demanding stamina were much beyond our expectations. In spite of the morning runs and skips there was no comparable improvement in the things which required spring, resilience or pure speed of reaction. This was not surprising because much of the activity in the boats and on the hills was not such as would contribute to this end. The improvement that was achieved in these events came simply from correction of faults, the development of sheer determination and hard practice. Over the longer distances, however, the performances were often astonishing and we concluded that the combined effect of heavy boat pulling, mountain walking and the general regime of vigorous activity was resulting in enhancement of stamina of a significant kind.

We were conscious of course of the danger of overstrain and a system of careful medical supervision had to be developed. Immediately each new course arrived the boys were examined by the local doctor, with whom we had entered into a special arrangement, and by Miss Wiltshire, our own Matron. Whenever there was any doubt about a boy's fitness for any part of the training a plan was made to ensure that he came under constant scrutiny. Miss Wiltshire showed great ingenuity in these matters. On occasions she suggested that a boy was slightly under weight and should attend daily at sick-bay for extra milk or cod liver oil. By this means she kept him under her eye as the demands of the training increasingly fell upon him. In extreme cases boys had to be returned to their homes. In other cases it would be clear that more than one course would be needed if the consequences of physical neglect were to be completely repaired.

One of the medical tests used at the beginning and end of each course was known as "tolerance to exercise." After having waited his turn for examination, seated and as relaxed as could be expected in the circumstances, the boy's pulse rate was discovered. He was then asked to carry out a standard exercise such as jumping on and off a chair a dozen times. His pulse rate was measured again immediately after the exercise and again after a further two-minute rest. Our experience seemed to indicate that those who recorded the lowest initial pulse rate, the smallest increase after exercise and the quickest return to normal were likely to prove by far the fittest and capable of much greater response to physical demands. Conversely, those with high initial rates and tendency to a marked increase after exercise were generally those whose way of life had contributed to a marked decline in fitness.

As time went by the matron developed a tendency to forecast the probable physical performances of boys whose tolerance to exercise figures seemed in any way abnormal. I recollect one most striking case. After a busy day of initial medical examinations Miss Wiltshire informed me that one of the boys would be likely to break our records for the two-mile run and the five-mile walk. It appeared that his tolerance test indicated quite exceptional stamina. I made a note of the boy's name. When I discovered him to be without doubt the thinnest, weediest youngster so far to present himself for the course, my first reaction was that Miss Wiltshire had been joking. This was not the case, however. She was convinced of the boy's potential. On Wednesday evening the boys were free to attend a dance in the village hall. The boy in question was due for punishment that evening for some comparatively trifling offence. A stock penalty was known as the "Pennal Walk." This involved a lonely walk after dinner to the village of Pennal — seven miles inland — where the vicar of the parish kindly maintained a book for signature by the miscreants.

I was surprised when this youngster asked my permission to attend the dance when he had completed his walk. It did not seem to me reasonable to expect him back before eleven o'clock and the sight of the boy on the dance floor halfway through the evening led me to suspect that he had cut short the trip or accepted a lift. This he denied; he had been all the way — completely on foot — and had signed the book. He admitted that he had done a bit of "trotting" to save time. There was, of course, no rule against this! Some time later I discovered that he had adopted one other time-saving device. The road inland from Abderdovey to Pennal follows the river and winds round a succession of rocky headlands. These the railway pierces in a series of tunnels. The boy had taken a torch and wherever the railway offered the shorter route, he had apparently run through the tunnel! One could not but admire both his courage (or disregard of danger) as well as his physical resources.

The Matron was correct. He did break our records for the longer distance events — apparently without effort.

While fitness was being improved by the daily activities attention was also being given to the technical skills essential to safe movement across country. Elementary instruction in the use of map and compass was carried out in the hills immediately to our north. These map reading walks were supplemented by longer excursions into the hills each Sunday. The culmination occurred during the final week-end of each course. By this time our own observation, coupled with the Matron's advice, enabled us to split the whole course into parties of five or six boys all at approximately equal levels of fitness. Each party was given its instructions early the previous evening so that the boys could work out the details of their routes and special equipment that might be needed, and so that they could seek advice on any matters on which they found themselves in doubt. During the final briefing we reiterated all they had been taught about party discipline and the techniques that are designed to promote safety in the mountains.

Early on the morning of the test the parties were dropped from train or bus at small halts to the west and north of the Cader Idris range. Each party's route would ensure that it was thoroughly separated from the others and forced to work out its own problems of route-finding in unfamiliar country. For the fittest, the day's walk would involve somewhere in the region of thirty miles over three distinct ranges including an aggregate climbing height of more than 5,000 feet. Even the less fit would undertake a journey varying from 15 to 25 miles and perhaps a total of 3,000 feet of climbing.

We used no routes until they had been reconnoitred by members of the staff so we were well aware of the hazards involved at different seasons of the year. On the occasion of the tests moreover we deployed our full strength of instructors to "check points" or places of observation from which we could verify that each party had safely negotiated each section of the route. It was of course vital in case of accident that we should know as precisely as possible in what areas to look for the injured or lost.

In course of time we flattered ourselves that we had reached a very high standard of care and precaution and we invited distinguished members of the Climbers' Club to investigate what we were doing and recommend any improvement in our instruction or safety precautions which they thought might prove helpful. We were acutely sensitive to the fact that an accident which might in any way be attributed to recklessness or negligence on our part would in all probability kill the whole enterprise in its absolute infancy. We were relieved therefore that the experts found generally in our favour. Roped rock climbing and similar activities were entirely outside our scope. We were concerned solely with route-finding and safe movement over difficult country coupled with the build-up of sheer endurance. Within these terms it was reported that generally our arrangements were sound enough. We gladly adopted such detailed suggestions as were made for improving our safety measures and acquired a complete set of mountain rescue equipment including a "Duff" stretcher on which casualties could be strapped and moved in a variety of ways. Underneath the stretcher were runners which permitted it to be used as a sledge or lowered down vertical or near vertical rock faces. Alternatively a single wheel could be clipped into position underneath thus making it possible on reasonably smooth ground to relieve the bearers of much dead weight and to move with considerable speed. An accompanying rucksack which was kept "at the ready" contained everything required for the first aid treatment of casualties. The use of this equipment added a valuable element to the training we offered to all the boys.

One day when expeditions were in progress I was stopped by a villager who told me that three of our boys had been killed in the mountains. Gradually many of our nearby hills had come into use for the training of Marines and other Commando troops. There was good evidence that they were leaving live ammunition and unexploded mortar bombs scattered over the ground and we were obliged to issue the direst warnings to our boys that such objects should in no circumstances be touched but that positions should be carefully noted for report to the military authorities. At last, it appeared, the worst had happened. The school rescue parties had left the school some time earlier when the news first came through. I drove to the point from which the parties would have struck to the hills. At the foot of Trum Gelli I took to my feet and soon saw a party bringing down a heavy burden on the Duff stretcher. It was shameful that one should feel so great a relief on discovering that the three victims were not our boys at all. They were the three young sons of a local farmer who, no doubt, had exploded a mortar bomb by striking it with a stone. Their bodies had been discovered by one of our expedition parties who thus presented our rescue services with a task of depressing sadness.

CHAPTER 10

The part of the training which proved most difficult to develop was that concerned with the small boats. While it is true that the Dovey estuary presents some very real dangers I could not help feeling that we were doing too little to overcome them. From the beginning it had seemed to me that we had to capture the boys' interest by the sheer pace and imagination of our programme. Once at the wharf, however, it was obvious that there was too much hanging about — a too leisurely preparation for each activity. What is more there was a marked reluctance to put the boys in a position of real command and initiative. Initially this was understandable. We had no powered craft of our own so that if anyone got into difficulties it would have been a lengthy business trying to reach them by cutter. Relatively early in our history, however, we were afforded some relief by the loan of a very handy launch Nestou II, the property of a businessman from the Midlands. Ideal for river work she was too lightly built and indeed underpowered for work in heavy seas. Nevertheless as a standby boat in the event of trouble in the estuary she was a most valuable acquisition.

We were further strengthened in due course by the arrival of another ship in the river. This was the Camroux, a coaster of about 500 tons which was to serve as a tender to a Ministry of Supply establishment which had been set up on the sand dunes at Borth, just across the river from us. She had a powered lifeboat which was most generously employed in our interests whenever need arose. All this increased our confidence and gradually we built up our own fleet of small craft.

Originally we had the two Gordonstoun cutters — one of dipping lug and the other of standing lug rig. The seamen all preferred the former. Bringing her about afforded the boys much greater opportunity for active participation in the sailing of the craft. In time therefore further drop-keel dipping lug cutters were built for us in Wales. All were fitted with tanks and were staunch and safe craft. We also brought down from Scotland a number of half-deckers and in other ways accumulated a variety of dinghies and small craft. The object was to give initial training to complete watches in the cutters — under oars and sail — and then as soon as possible and conditions permitted to get the boys away in the dinghies and half-deckers without officers so that they could learn from their own mistakes.

There was an elaborate system of safety precautions. No one was allowed in small boats without a life jacket. No boats were allowed to leave the wharf unless look-outs had been posted, the motor of the launch had been run-up and tested and the duty officer was known to be on hand. No officer was permitted to take charge of a boat with boys in it until he had familiarised himself with the character of the estuary and demonstrated his personal competence. There was an occasion when this last restriction was ignored with memorable consequences.

We were always seeking to widen our sources of recruitment and Laurence Holt and his associates spared no effort to make our work known throughout the world of shipping. On one occasion we were visited by Captain Russell, the Marine Superintendent of the Anglo-Saxon Line. It was of the utmost importance that we should impress him favourably. In the afternoon of this visit the conditions seemed almost ideal for sailing. A fresh westerly wind countered an ebbing tide. The word was passed round for maximum concentration at the wharf. Soon all boats were away but one — a small dinghy brought by Gordonstoun from Scotland and named, in honour of their boat-builder there, the Alexander Findlay. Unfortunately her reputation at Aberdovey did little honour to the worthy Scot. Everyone spoke of her as a "cranky" boat and she was always the last to be chosen.

Standing disgruntled on the wharf was a young Dutch second officer who had just joined us. He begged to be allowed to take the sole remaining dinghy to join what was positively a cavalcade of small craft on the river. I explained our rule. None of us had seen him sail; the boat was tricky in the extreme. I was sorry.

He took this extraordinarily hard. He pointed out that our precautions might be necessary for Englishmen, who naturally had little opportunity to acquire boat sense. But Dutchmen were apparently born in boats. It was a positive insult to cast any doubt on their capacity to handle small craft of any description. Reluctantly I agreed that he should take two boys in the Alexander Findlay.

Meanwhile Captain Russell was exulting in the sight that lay before him. Immediately alongside the wharf lay the Prince Louis. She was always a pretty sight. Beyond, scattered over the estuary, we had close on a dozen and a half craft — everything we could muster, including the schooner's two lifeboats also under sail. I swelled with pride. This was salesmanship with a vengeance. Below us the Dutch officer completed the rigging of the dinghy and struck out round the end of the wharf and into the main stream. As he cleared the schooner he beat quickly downstream and then came about. It dawned upon me that he was closing in on the ship far too swiftly and would have no alternative but to gybe on to a change of course. This was a manoeuvre one carried out with considerable caution in the Alexander Findlay. Surely enough she heeled straight over and capsized in the very forefront of public view.

With great speed the other boats came to the rescue. One cutter took the officer and the two boys from the water. Another secured the dinghy and towed it ashore where it was turned over and drained out. In the meantime, the bosun of the schooner, who was sailing our fastest boat, a half-rater called the Sea Swallow, tacked down river smartly recovering floorboards, rudder, tiller and oars. In twenty minutes the Findlay was complete and back in the water. Captain Russell danced with excitement. He found it all totally irresistible and his company was soon one of our most loyal customers.

Efforts on my part to change the character of our waterborne activities were frustrated by my own ignorance of the techniques involved. There appeared to be only one course open. I resolved to find out for myself. One evening when I thought myself unobserved I selected what I thought to be the smallest and simplest of the boats available and cast off. Alas, a sluggish and fast falling westerly breeze was no match for the ebbing tide. Slowly but surely I lost ground. Though heading up river I was making steady progress towards the bar. Efforts to row back to the wharf were frustrated by a faulty rowlock. In shame I steered to the shore and set about the humiliating task of towing the boat home. It was then that I discovered that my antics had been observed and noted. My further efforts were even more unfortunate and it was necessary to look in other directions for improvement.

A time came when we were used for certain experiments in survival at sea. As new types of lifeboats were developed we received prototypes and experienced officers were sent to carry out sea tests for which our boys supplied the crews. We also tested other appliances. After publicity had been given to the use of an improvised still for the distillation of sea water a number of research projects were mounted in an effort to develop a serviceable still for use in lifeboats and even on rafts. As the prototypes became available we tested them under realistic conditions. For the boys, unfortunately, these ventures meant little more than hard pulling over the bar and hours of sailing in cold and exposed conditions outside. No doubt they were impressed by the endurance of the solitary officer who sat it out hour after hour on a raft, carefully checking his distillation rates as he rolled and pitched at his moorings by the bar and they visited him at intervals to make sure that he was still there. But even these diversions did not constitute what some of us felt to be the kind of activities which would stretch and stir the individual boy who came to us. For advance on this front we had to await the arrival and growing influence of two men, each of whom in his special way contributed enormously to our development.

Freddie Fuller was sent to us early in 1943 by the Blue Funnel Line. At that time he was a second mate and he had just survived a double hazard. When his ship was torpedoed in the South Atlantic and all the boats had left, the vessel continued to float. He returned to the ship only to be shelled by the attacking submarine. Even his own lifeboat then sought to put a safe distance between itself and the doomed ship, so that Freddie and his three companions were forced to launch a small boat from the poop. When he regained his lifeboat he commanded it for 35 days, maintaining order among a heterogeneous crew, eking out the rations and supplementing them with collected rainwater. At the end of this time they were rescued by a British tramp steamer which itself, in turn, was torpedoed only a week later. Fortunately Freddie's second spell in a lifeboat lasted only two days when he was rescued again, this time by a Barbados schooner which landed him in Georgetown, British Guiana. At the time he was thirty years of age and seemed an obvious choice to pass the benefit of his experience to others.

About Freddie's skill in boats, practical ability and leadership amongst the boys there was no doubt whatever. Unlike so many competent seamen who had been at the school he knew what would capture the interest and imagination of young men. When he arrived, however, we had a strong contingent of Captains attached to the school — one in charge of Bryneithyn, one at the wharf, and two for the sea-going craft. Bound by the protocol of the service Freddie chafed at his inability to break through to less conservative methods of training. I have no doubt that he held me personally responsible for much that he found unsatisfactory and for a long time I stood between two powerful forces — the stolidity of the Captains, many of whom were charming men, and the dynamic force of a young officer who regarded most established institutions with scant respect. It was a novel experience for me to act as peacemaker and to find myself actually defending those who found it difficult to amend their practices.

Effective backing for Freddie Fuller came from an unexpected source. It had always seemed to us that we ought to enjoy the support of the Admiralty as a supplement to the pre-sea training offered in the Sea Cadet Corps. Eventually they arranged for a formal inspection of our work. The officer appointed for this task was Commander T. G. Bedwell who acted as an adviser on pre-entry training to the Admiral Commanding Reserves. Bedwell proved an extremely gracious guest. Not only did he commend what we were doing but he saw the very great possibilities of improvement. His report to the Admiralty presented our efforts in glowing terms. He considered the Admiralty should use us to the full but refrain from attempting to control our methods.

So impressed were the directors with Bedwell's comments on the school that very shortly he joined the board with a special responsibility for advising on training methods. This was a tremendous advantage. Bedwell, in the midst of a very busy life, spent as much time as he could afford at Aberdovey, greatly strengthening all efforts to inject an active adventurous element into the small boat work. He also became one of our most energetic "outside representatives" and a great deal of new recruitment was the result of the enthusiastic account he gave of our activities as he visited Sea Cadet units and industrial concerns up and down the country.

From this time forward the quality of the training in seamanship was to be steadily improved. Bedwell saw the full possibilities of our situation and his authority to galvanise the work was strengthened when he was formally nominated Director of Training. Shortly afterwards Fuller became Chief Executive Officer; together they prepared schemes of seamanship training and both began to exert an influence on all aspects of the life of the school.

CHAPTER 11

After the alarming episodes which marked the early cruises of the Prince Louis, a succession of Captains took over the command and each made his own contribution to the emerging pattern of training. All who came had gained experience early in their careers of the operation of sailing craft. Since then, however, they had spent many years in steamships and could be forgiven if they viewed with misgiving the task of sailing a small and lively schooner close in to the coastline hazards of Cardigan Bay. Of those who first overcame their apprehension at this task I remember particularly Captain "Jimmy" Nelson. He coupled a genial personality with superb mastery of his craft. The schooner reflected the change of command as soon as he took it over. Previously painted black she was soon re-dressed in pale grey and white and all her fittings and rigging were re-furbished so that we all took pride in her appearance. But performance matched the care and skill in preparation and she was soon carrying out her duties with such regularity that it became the rule rather than the exception for the majority of the boys to complete a cruise during the course.

Captain John Power was another who commanded the ship with complete confidence and the need for this quality became more marked as new hazards were added to the natural difficulties of the bay. During the progress of the war more and more military units opened up training activities around the perimeter of our cruising area.

Immediately south of the river at Borth was a Ministry of Supply proof-range where various new weapons were put to test. Thus we witnessed the trials of rockets fired from the land to the sea, from rocket ships to the sand dunes and from aircraft into the waters of the estuary. I do not recall these interfering seriously with our own activities. At Towyn was based an R.A.S.C. unit training crews in the operation of amphibious craft known as DUKWS or "Ducks" as we called them, which merely added to the obstacles to be negotiated by novices in the estuary itself.

Also at Towyn was an R.A.F. station operating "Queen Bees" (radio controlled target aircraft) and towing drogue targets for the training of anti-aircraft gunners at Tonfanau a little to the north. Further north still, at Harlech, anti-tank gunnery was practised by firing out to sea. Further still round the north of the bay near Pwllheli was an R.A.F. bombing school.

Each time the schooner put to sea it traversed the ranges of these units and there was no guarantee that visibility would be such that its presence would be noted. It became my duty not only to obtain confidential weather reports before each sailing but also to notify the officers commanding many of the units concerned of our movements. With a sailing ship, however, it was not always possible to adhere closely to a predetermined schedule and there were occasions when things took on an ugly tinge.

Shells from the anti-tank guns at Harlech were frequently alleged to have passed very close to the ship. Much as I was tempted to take some accounts with a pinch of salt it was difficult to ignore the alarm of Captain Evans who claimed that a shell had passed through the rigging of the schooner. For days he muttered unceasingly, "Right through the damn rigging! I ask you. It's going too far."

I myself experienced the sensation of being under fire. The schooner had just cast off her moorings when we received a telephone message informing us that the father of one of her officers was seriously ill and the son's presence in Glasgow was urgently required. By the time I reached the wharf the ship was well on her way to the bar. It seemed I might catch her by taking the launch; Nestou II. had enough petrol for what was likely to be a short trip and the weather was perfectly fair and settled.

By the time I reached the bar the Prince Louis was under full sail and had a lead of over a mile. My only hope was that I should be sighted and that she would come about for me. What actually happened was that she supplemented sail with both engines in order to clear as quickly as possible the Tonfanau firing range. As she did so the gunners re-opened fire on the drogue which was being towed above me and a hail of shrapnel commenced. The launch was a single clinker-built shell and one piece would have sufficed to send her to the bottom. What was equally worrying was that the petrol indicator was falling steadily. Either I had to catch the ship and take on fresh fuel or turn back very quickly indeed. Having decided to carry on I was fortunate that after an unconscionable delay I was sighted and the schooner lay to for me to fetch up with her .With full tanks and the comfort of a

Kurt Hahn on board the 'Prince Louis' on her arrival at Aberdovey from Scotland. Summer 1941.

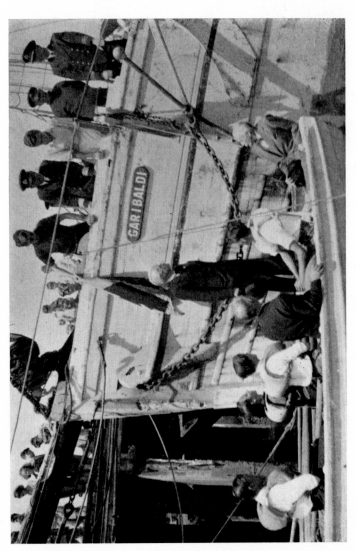

Outward Bound, Aberdovey.
Christening of the 'Garibaldi.'
In cutter: Laurence Holt, George Trevelyan, Geoffrey Winthrop Young.

THE WARDENS 1967.

Photo: Glyn Davies

E. W. Dawson
(Exec. Director)

Tom Price, B.A.
(Eskdale)

Captain J. F. Fuller, M.B.E.
(Aberdovey)

Major Gordon Richards, M.B.E.
(Moray)

Lt. Col. Ian Frazer, M.B.E.
(Devon)

Squad. Leader Lester Davis, F.R.G.S.
(Ullswater)

Miss Anne Cordiner
(Rhowniar)

Outward Bound, Aberdovey.
Dr. Zimmerman, Laurence Holt, the Author, C. Sparks.

Outward Bound, Eskdale.
The House and the Tarn.

Photo: Jim Davis

Outward Bound, Ullswater.
Winter Expeditions.

Photo: Bob Godfrey

City Challenge, 1967.
Building the Adventure Playground.

Outward Bound, Devon
Launching for Surf Canoeing.

Photo: Bristol Evening Post.

companion on the return journey I ran the Tonfanau gauntlet somewhat more confidently.

The worst instance of the unreliability of the sailing craft occurred at Christmas in 1942. The schooner was in need of an under-water repair for which time was necessary. Simple jobs could be carried out at Aberdovey by bringing her onto the inner side of the wharf which dried out completely between tides. On this occasion ,however, we faced a more serious matter and had to compete for the use of a dry dock, all of which were then in constant demand for service ships.

After negotiation we booked a suitable dock at Port Dinorwic in the Menai Straits for the period immediately before Christmas. It was easy to recruit a volunteer crew from the outgoing course, but when the sailing date dawned the weather was forbidding. Heavy seas were already breaking on the bar and the weather forecast promised a southerly gale. The prospect of losing our long-sought booking drove us to attempt the passage. Before we reached the bar the boy crew had passed out, the Captain had prudently gone below to remove his teeth and it was obvious we were in for a rough time. Throughout the day the weather worsened and as the light failed we were scarcely clear of Bardsea Sound. There was no hope of reaching the Menai Straits and it fell dark as we groped into shelter in the rock-bound bay off Morfa Nevin. For two days we idled there while a vicious gale blew itself out.

Haunted by thoughts of the mounting work at Aberdovey I decided to desert ship on the morning of the day the schooner was to resume her passage. In the inky blackness of a December morning I descended to the ship's boat which was to put me ashore. Shortly after casting off I became conscious of water rising in the bottom of the boat. Some youngster had omitted to put the bung in! Standing cold, wet-footed and completely unorientated on a dark and dismal beach I contemplated the slender prospects of obtaining transport. As I started to plod through the soggy sand there came into sight what appeared to be the headlights of a car driving along the beach itself. My fears mounted that I might be shot as an unauthorised invader before I could explain my presence. The car approached and stopped. It was the officer commanding balloon barrages in Wales and I had secured myself a lift.

The schooner reached Port Dinorwic in time for the boys to rush home for Christmas. The repair completed, the crew rejoined and set out on the return trip. Unfortunately bad weather returned too and just out of the Menai Straits her main gaff carried away. She turned about immediately for a further repair. The second time she set out for home another gale blew up and she was forced into St. Tydwall's for a sheltered anchorage. In all she was away from Aberdovey for several weeks.

Difficulties multiplied as we started to accept larger numbers of boys. By 1943 we were expecting courses of more than a hundred boys. It was patently impossible to take all of those to sea with only one ship. Efforts were made to discover a second vessel, preferably of the same general capacity but of lower draught. As usual Alfred Holt and Company acted as guardians of our interests. A French ketch was refitted to suit our purposes and equipped with a powerful engine. With a draught of some nine and a half as opposed to the schooner's eleven and a half feet she promised to be a particularly valuable acquisition.

On the 26th June, 1943, the new craft was re-named the Garibaldi by the Master of Trinity, Professor G. M. Trevelyan. He was supported by Geoffrey Winthrop Young, President of the Alpine Club. The two short speeches made on this occasion perfectly express the principles which were steadily emerging as the basis of all our work. For this reason it seems fitting that they should be reproduced in full.

After a brief introduction by Laurence Holt, George Trevelyan spoke as follows:

I have been asked to baptise this ketch by the name of "Garibaldi," the sea-captain, who became the greatest of all practitioners in that peculiar art which we may call "revolutionary war."

His qualities of adventurous leadership were trained as only a sailing ship can train them. We want as many boys as possible to have that training. It has been one of the peculiar merits of Gordonstoun School to supply that spirit. For that reason Gordonstoun was able to provide the Navy at the beginning of the war with lads of nautical experience, who have since done great things in the Dover Patrol and elsewhere. And now the Outward Bound Sea School is carrying on the good work on a still larger scale, in the interests of the nation as a whole.

The life of the Training Ship and the discpline of the sea give an education in qualities that are current also by land, as the case of Garibaldi shows — the qualities of endurance, promptitude and love of adventure. Without the instinct for adventure in young men, any civilisation, however enlightened, any state, however well ordered, must wilt and wither. Thank God our young men have shown in the last three years that, however modern they may be, they still have the spirit of adventure, and display it in all the three elements in which war is now waged. And like Garibaldi, they are not wasting that spirit of adventure for selfish puposes, but like him dedicate it to the battle for the freedom of their country and for the freedom of the whole world.

"Garibawldi" our simple ancestors called him — the correct Italian pronunciation is Garibaldi. Call him which you will. He laid a solemn curse on any Italian who should ever fight against England, the champion of Italy's freedom and the world's. That curse is now falling on Mussolini, the man who has for the last twenty years been trying by force to educate the Italian people out of the humane and liberal ideals of Garibaldi into a despotic and cruel creed of his own invention.

After his sea-training in the Mediterranean, Garibaldi spent a dozen years in South America, sailing along its coasts and riding over the great spaces of its then virgin pampas, where he learnt the arts of guerilla war among the half-civilised cavalry of those regions, which in those days were seldom at peace. With such an upbringing you might have expected the revolutionary warrior of Italy to be himself a rough customer with a touch of the gangster. But in fact one of Garibaldi's most striking features, in war and peace, was his tender humanity to friend and to foe, to men and to animals. A touch of St. Francis of Assisi was strangely mingled with his other more formidable qualities.

To men of other lands and most of all to us Englishmen, Garibaldi will remain as the incarnate symbol of two passions, not likely to die out of the world, love of country and love of liberty, kept pure by the one thing which can tame yet not weaken them, tender humanity for all men.

This ketch is named "The Garibaldi."

Immediately after the naming of the ketch Geoffrey Winthrop Young followed:

Twice in a lifetime we have seen war produce in quite ordinary men and women heroic qualities of courage, endurance and self-sacrifice and make permanently better citizens of those whom it did not destroy. And twice we, who have been concerned with education, have had to recognise that our ordinary systems of education had failed to educe those chivalrous qualities, in any considerable degree, in peace time.

To realise his better self everyone must pass in youth through some test of adventure and hardship and the adventure must be real; a conflict with the natural environment and yet it must be adjustable, so as not to overtax adolescence. The forces of nature alone provide these natural adventures and tests of personality: the winds, the roughened surface of the sea, and the rough hill surface of the land.

For centuries our people have been learning their manhood from our surrounding sea, from its uncertain adventure and stern discipline. Some of us, like myself, have during the past century discovered the lessons that are to be learned from the mountains, from their mystery, romance and hardship. And now at last, and under the stresses of these great wars, we have been learning slowly whence we must draw those disciplines for manhood which our organised education in peace has never yet supplied.

We made a beginning between the wars and Gordonstoun School gave us the leading example of how sea-faring, coast-watching and such real responsibilities can be made a part of the training of the young. Other experiments upon the same lines are being inaugurated, such as the badge scheme and the proposed use of our hills for holiday training camps, and even in the stress of the present war this Outward Bound Sea School has carried the application of the idea one great stride forward.

This sailing ship, now dedicated to the service of the Sea School, we have today christened "The Garibaldi." And rightly so, for Garibaldi was a sailor who pre-eminently used the lessons of his long and hard sea training for the great task of the freeing of his country. In so doing he became an example for all Europe and for all time, of the qualities of self-devotion, endurance, and chivalry, which are called for by the right service of a State and essential to the attainment of its ordered freedom.

CHAPTER 12

Immediately the ceremony of re-naming the ketch was completed the Prince Louis and the Garibaldi cast off and were escorted to the bar by twelve of the small craft. Henceforward there was less difficulty in keeping our promise to give to all who came to us at least a taste of life at sea in a sailing vessel. Furthermore, as the ships normally sailed in escort a variety of training exercises arose out of the simple process of communication between the two — by signals when under way and by boat work when at their anchorages.

The boys became the crews of the ships in a very real sense. All the heaving on the capstans and hauling on the heavy sails fell to them. If they wished to eat, someone had to face the ordeal of cooking in the confined and lurching galleys right in the forepeaks of both craft. Anchor watch at night afforded a sense of genuine responsibility for the safety of all on board and also, for many town-bred boys, the first experience of standing completely alone under the night sky. In spite of all, however, I came to feel real doubts about the claims that were made for this aspect of our work.

The operation of the ships was governed entirely by the weather, coupled with the state of the tides. There were occasions when if the schooner did not sail within a day or so of the commencement of a course she would be "neaped" and lose a week of sailing opportunity. In any case it was unavoidable that the watches that went to sea early in the course would do so with very little preliminary training. Instead of the sea cruise serving as the culmination of a process of preparation, for some it became a rude introduction to the course as a whole. Furthermore the entire character of the experience was completely outside our control. There were times in summer when the ships made delightful passages in light winds and glorious sunshine. Boys could spend much of their leisure sun-bathing on deck or trailing mackerel lines over the stern. In winter, however, there were occasions when the ships corkscrewed and spiralled their way through heavy seas and when the freezing gear had to be handled in conditions of near misery. Nor was it possible to control the onslaught of sea-sickness. I can recall occasions when the crew of twelve boys lay awash in the scuppers on the lee-side prepared to drown rather than rouse themselves from their stupor. Reports on a boy's disposition to service in these circumstances take on an element of unreality.

There was one other matter which forced me to question the educational value of this part of the course. A succession of Captains took command of the ships, each arriving for a respite from the strain of normal war-time duty. Many were men of sterling quality, often survivors of most testing experiences at sea. They were not chosen however for their knowledge of, or sympathy with, the young. The first responsibility of the Captain was the safe operation of the ship. In such circumstances it was easy for the boys to be regarded merely as 'crew.' Many officers did their best to provide a variety of experience and to explain to the boys all their decisions and the grounds on which they were taken. But some were totally out of sympathy with our purposes and a few had standards of personal behaviour which it would have been difficult to justify to anyone who chose to complain. Ultimately it was this issue which convinced me that my usefulness at Aberdovey had been exhausted. Our progress in other fields occasioned us far less anxiety.

The original plan in Hahn's mind had been to demonstrate the effectiveness of the County Badge idea as a challenge to endeavour. Certainly I had myself planned the sea school programme around the concept of the "Fourfold Achievement." Outward Bound Badges were awarded to those who attained set standards in physical tests, a project of technical skill and knowledge, an expedition (including, if possible a sea passage), and the responsible discharge of specified tasks of service. An additional condition was that the boy should have accepted and observed certain training conditions.

In practice this produced unfairness. However much we might try to adjust our demands to the potential of each boy there were some who found success relatively easy of achievement. Boys of good intelligence accustomed to applying themselves to the task of learning had obvious advantages. If, in addition, they were physically fit and athletically gifted they could go through the whole course with great distinction whereas their less fortunate companions in spite of commendable efforts might fail in the time to overcome all of their difficulties. From the beginning we were conscious that the badge system would prove an embarrassment unless re-assessed in the light of our special circumstances.

There were two points of view about the steps we should take. We could leave things as they were, asserting that our intention had been merely to demonstrate a method and to give boys such a taste of success that they might be expected to continue their training elsewhere. Indeed we encouraged them to do this and awarded a number of badges to boys whose final tests were passed and certified in their own schools or youth organisations. The number who did this however was small and was likely to remain so simply because so many boys went straight from Aberdovey into various forms of national service.

The second point of view was that the course should be regarded as a self-contained experience and that boys should be judged simply on their performance while they were with us. Even though I was personally committed to the furtherance of the County Badge idea, continued observation of the boys who came into our care compelled me to favour some compromise. People are more important than systems and we were living in vital relationships with a succession of youngsters, many of whom commanded our lively admiration. In the light of experience we modified standards so as to take account of what normal boys would reasonably be expected to achieve in four weeks of hard endeavour. Even so only about half of all who came succeeded in reaching what we termed our "Standard" badge, and about one in twenty gained the "Silver," which was an achievement of real distinction. We could not send away half of our trainees, many of whom had stretched themselves to their limits, without recognition of their often splendid efforts. Thus we came to evolve a new concept in which the "Membership Badge" was awarded to all who passed through the course satisfactorily without regard to specific standards of attainment. This shift of emphasis made us free to concentrate to a greater degree on what we were coming to recognise as by far the most exciting aspect of our work. Important as it might be to help each boy to achieve some success in a limited task of training there were other experiences the consequences of which were no less significant.

For many boys this was the first prolonged absence from home and familiar surroundings. Some had to be led through a period of acute homesickness and difficult adjustment. It was very rarely indeed that we failed to persuade them to give it all a fair trial and once past the first week the initial problem was usually resolved.

Each course threw up a very wide cross-section of the nation.

Amongst those who intended to make a career at sea for example, there were potential deck officers, deck hands, trainee stewards, carpenters and engineers. Some were the products of good grammar and public schools often followed by a period at such well-known schools as H.M.S. Conway, Pangbourne or Worcester. The engineer apprentices, too, would have continued their education in technical colleges. The overwhelming majority of these youngsters were of good intelligence, accustomed to the disciplines of learning, generally (though not always) sympathetic to our general purposes and for the most part disposed to be co-operative. Furthermore, many of them were prepared to shoulder the responsibility of making decisions and persuading others to accept them. The trainee deck hands and stewards in some instances presented an entirely different problem. Amongst them were many who were far from bright. It was sadly obvious that their background of home and school had left them pessimistic about their capabilities, on guard against the risk of exposing their inadequacies, often timid and suspicious if not positively hostile.

One could identify similar elements amongst those who were not destined for careers at sea. On the one hand there were the boys who were privately sponsored, possibly from wealthy and cultured homes and, on the other, youngsters sent by industrial concerns or local education authorities. These were often excellent lads chosen no doubt because they had merited special consideration. Some firms, however, were wise enough to send their "problem" youngsters, to see if we could do anything to infect them with a new set of values or sense of purpose.

At the beginning of each course we took very great trouble indeed in allocating the boys to their "watches" to make sure that as far as we could make it so each group of twelve would reflect a fair cross-section of the course as a whole. Not only was it necessary to distribute the potential leaders; it was also imperative to scatter those who were likely to need a great deal of support and encouragement as well as those who might be highly resistant. Originally this was seen as a simple problem of organising efficiently for a straightforward educational task. As time went by however our perspective changed. It became clear to some of us that in welding totally disparate elements into a close-knit and loyal team a process was taking place which might be very much more significant than the grade of badge for which a boy might qualify. Repeatedly one saw intimate friendships established between boys from totally different backgrounds. Frequently this sprang from the growth of mutual respect arising out of testing situations. Certainly until this process got well under way each course was a struggle.

The thing that one remembers most clearly is not the process of teaching new skills but the wrestling to produce more mature understanding and tolerance. I recall the long drawn-out effort to convince a young watch captain — intellectually able and physically well endowed — that neither arrogance on his part nor violence would in any way improve the behaviour of an unfortunate youth in his watch whose whole background had contributed to make him weedy, devious and unlikeable. On the other hand unplanned circumstances often did what we would have wished to do but had not the skill to devise. One intending seaman came from serving as a pot boy in an East End pub to face the ordeal of our demanding regime. Small, self-effacing and pathetically humble, he was patronised by all and showed no signs of resenting it. He was one of a watch of twelve who formed the schooner's crew on a particularly unpleasant passage. By a pure quirk of Providence he was entirely unaffected by the sickness which obliterated his companions. Throughout the trip he manned the galley, producing hot meals and drinks for the officers and himself, and regularly patrolled the lee side of the ship so as to re-distribute those of his comrades who were disposed to lie drowning in the scuppers, which were well awash.

As things got worse his cheerfulness — not to say cockiness— visibly increased. When the watch shamefacedly struggled back to consciousness the old relationships were patently inappropriate. Not only was he treated with respect; he was in fact a changed person and he did not look back. Previously the pet of the watch, henceforth he accepted the role of potential bulwark.

Conscious as one is of the extent to which our national life is affected by the suspicions and resentments of a class-divided society, the evidence of a breaching of the barriers seemed to us to be of the greatest importance. The boys were by no means slow to appreciate that in moments of crisis or in the long drawn out exposure to danger or sheer fatigue what really counts is the other chap's inner resources, staying power — and unselfishness. And they perceived that there was no invariable correlation between what was needed and the particular background from which a boy was drawn.

It was not only that boys were given the chance to assess other people in situations of strain. They could not fail to re-assess themselves. There must have been few who viewed all of the activities with equanimity. Month after month as I gave the introductory talk and outlined what would be expected before the end, I was conscious of the politely restrained derision and incredulity with which it was all received. Yet equally, month after month, the magic somehow worked and each normal sample of young men grew visibly in confidence and determination. In some cases the effect was dramatic; the intensity of experience undoubtedly caused a boy to face life with a new spirit and attitude. More often however one was well content to know that a boy had been caused to "raise his sights," to believe that given faith in himself and the courage to face a situation he was capable of more than previously he had conceived as possible.

Certainly this must have been the impression gained by many who sent boys on the courses. Recruitment at first was from a narrow front — Gordonstoun, Conway, and Alfred Holt and Company. Gradually the net was widened. Other merchant shipping lines, the larger industrial concerns with adventurous training policies, independent schools, and certain local education authorities were slowly added to the list. Hahn, Bedwell and others spoke and wrote constantly of our work. Our activities were newsworthy and we featured often in the press and film magazines. Those whose interest had been thus alerted came to see for themselves whether our services were likely to afford good value. It was gratifying that as our customers grew in number we had no difficulty in retaining the originals.

I spent a good deal of time talking to industrialists, Rotary clubs, and educational gatherings. Generally it was not difficult to gain goodwill. Particularly in war-time the great majority of people seemed sympathetic to the general nature both of our purposes and our practices. Nevertheless there were many whose sensible scepticism caused them to doubt whether an experience packed into one month could really prove of lasting value. Frequently people enquired whether we had conducted any kind of "follow-up" investigation. This was ruled out for a large number who went almost immediately into the armed forces. In face of repeated enquiry, however, we devised a simple questionnaire which might be sent to employers, and for a time arranged for this to be issued six months after the completion of each course. The replies were generally most favourable. I can recall only one which was frankly critical. It came from an elderly and exceedingly blunt Yorkshire employer who had insisted on staying with us for several days before making up his mind whether we were likely to offer good value for money. After sending some two or three boys he decided against us. In his view the ones who were selected for this experience became somewhat "uppish" and unsettled. Apparently their ambitions had been stimulated and there was some danger that they would contemplate leaving the firm. Worst of all, the one who worked in the office constantly demanded that the windows should be opened. In Sheffield that must have been excessively tiresome!

I remember two cases which I personally found very encouraging. In the course of his unceasing advocacy of our interests Commander Bedwell, our Director of Training, had for a long time completely failed to move a fellow employer who might have opened an important source of recruitment. Finally, Bedwell broke through. One boy was sent as a test case but Bedwell's private information revealed that it would be a test of considerable stringency. I was not allowed to alert my colleagues but I was warned that the boy was on the verge of a "sacking." Having started as an apprentice and enjoyed all the advantages of day release for technical studies and a planned scheme of training, his total irresponsibility led to his gradual demotion. At that time he was washing cars in the firm's garage under threat that any further trouble would ensure his final removal from the scene.

Naturally I expected a tough trouble-maker and was astounded to find instead a highly delightful youngster: flaxen curly hair crowned a happy open face. I concluded that Bedwell had been pulling my leg — or someone had been pulling his. Not for the first time, I was forced to discount first impressions. On the first day the young "innocent" was hauled before the court of watch captains who were responsible for normal disciplinary matters. He became a regular attender there and a regular pounder of the road to Pennal and back. It was not that he was wicked but rather that he was feckless and totally unashamed.

At the end of the course I wrote to Bedwell confessing failure. There was no evidence that we had made the slightest impression on this youngster.

Some months later I sent the stock questionnaire to his employers — with foreboding. The reply said that he was still employed. There had been no further trouble with him and it was known to the firm that he had resumed attendance at the technical college, voluntarily and for evening classes only. They had already determined that if he succeeded in this way he would be re-instated as an apprentice.

The second case concerned a boy employed in the London office of a shipping company. That he had ability there was no doubt but his own certainty on this point was offensively obvious. Officers complained to me of his insolence and general unhelpfulness. When I discussed these difficulties with him I felt a complete lack of progress. He seemed coldly self-assured and unresponsive. Again when he left I thought we had failed to make any useful contribution to the boy's development.

About a year later the B.B.C. asked if I could suggest a boy who could take part in a radio discussion. It was essential that he should have been through a course at the school, could be released during working hours and should have an accent or dialect which was sharply distinctive.

As it was difficult to keep contact with boys after they left, the number who leapt to mind was strictly limited. However I had been told by the employers of the young Londoner that he had profited greatly from the course. I rang them up and they were enthusiastic. I asked if they would send him to Aberdovey for a week-end so that he might see what new developments had occurred since he left. I also wished to satisfy myself about the improvement that had been claimed in the boy's attitudes. It was all arranged and I had extended conversations with him.

He was a keen member of a Sea Cadet unit and before he came to us he had been used exclusively as "the writer" of the unit. His office training had made him useful in tackling the clerical and administrative chores. He had resented his exclusion from normal training activities and from the usual stages of promotion. When he had returned from Aberdovey he had strongly argued that the training in practical seamanship had made him far more useful in other spheres and consequently he had been permitted to take a leading part in the normal work of the unit.

Before coming to Aberdovey he had regarded himself as an athletic "rabbit." Under Zimm's treatment he had discovered no little talent and, unknown to us, had resolved to continue his training when he left. This he had done by regularly running to and from his work in the City! But, as is usually the case, enthusiasm of this kind has to be communicated. He had persuaded other members of the Sea Cadets to join him in training and had pressed his officers to allow the unit to put a team into the district Youth Sports in which they had previously taken no part. The officers offered no objection if the boy was prepared to accept all the responsibility involved. He had done this and led his team to victory. Much more important was the effect of all this on the boy himself. One began to see how much he had resented the relegation to the ranks of the "swots" — the studious ones who are thought to be ineffective in the life of action.

The things that had happened in these two cases had occurred without our knowledge. We could not claim that they were the anticipated results of skilful planning. They had happened however — and in cases about which we had felt despondent. "Success" in education is difficult to assess and it may even be dangerous to attempt to measure it. Nevertheless, we could not help being conscious that we were privileged to participate in a process which could have effects such as I have described. But the more one pondered consequences of this significance in the lives of other people the more one was forced to weigh one's responsibility and re-state one's priorities of concern.

CHAPTER 13

I had drawn great enjoyment and satisfaction from what had been accomplished. There was, however, plenty of ground for dissatisfaction. The scatter of our accommodation did little to help us in the task of integrating a series of disparate communities and the makeshift nature of much of our furniture and equipment did nothing to promote such graciousness of environment as we would have wished to afford to some of the less fortunate of our youngsters. These were matters which, as long as the war lasted, were totally outside our control. There were other directions in which I felt that improvement ought to be made, but progress was agonisingly slow.

In the early days of the school I was the only full-time member of the staff directly concerned with training. After a few months Zimmermann was recognised as a permanent addition. Apart from the two of us, all others were on secondment for varying periods from Alfred Holt and Company. Economically this was ideal, but there was one great drawback. None of the people who came to us could be expected to feel profound loyalty to the school or any strong sense of mission towards the job that had to be done. Many plunged into the task with zeal and effectiveness but too often they had to be withdrawn as soon as they had gained worthwhile experience. A considerable number were seriously unsuited to the work we had to do.

From time to time I found myself having to suggest to Laurence Holt that one or other of the men he was so generously putting at our disposal was hardly the kind one would choose to have in an educational situation of an unusually exacting kind. Mr. Holt patiently explained the difference in our viewpoints and motives. He conceded that I must be concerned primarily to do a good job for the boys. He felt himself obliged to think also of the effect the school might have on his officers. A man who was being groomed for promotion, for instance, might learn much of patience and understanding by being called upon to nurse a watch of boys through all their trials and difficulties. In return we gained from the professional skill and knowledge such a man could bring to our service. In reply to such an argument it always seemed the height of ingratitude to point out that in certain circumstances one aim might totally frustrate the other.

Not all of the seconded officers were on the threshold of new responsibilities. Some had undergone experiences at sea which had undermined their confidence; some had blundered professionally or revealed signs of weaknesses which, unchecked, might destroy their careers. It was typical of Laurence Holt's generosity of spirit that he should want to do all in his power to help his men back to full health and vigour. And it was embarrassing for us that he had a touching faith in our capacity to assist in the healing and strengthening process. Unfortunately there were times when I felt that the refusal to concentrate on our first obligation would bring us to ignominious failure in both. I pointed out that in any normal educational establishment every care would be devoted to selecting people for the particular role they were to play. One could never expect a complete team of enthusiasts but a sound core of permanent staff would carry a minority of the uncommitted. In Aberdovey, however, the permanent people constituted a very small minority and it was utterly unreasonable to expect even the best disposed of the nomads to exert a great deal of influence on some of the unpromising men who were sent to us.

Things were made even more difficult by the hierarchy of rank within the shipping company. It was perhaps inevitable that generally it was the younger men who adapted themselves most readily and were most useful in the real business of training. Frequently progress, in the educational sense, was frustrated by older and more senior officers whose sympathies had not been won.

Laurence Holt was completely unimpressed by these difficulties. All I could gain from him was an assurance that whenever things got too bad he would come down himself to put matters right. Any suggestion of increasing the permanent staff so as to ease the task was turned down quite flatly as being calculated to weaken "the living link with the sea." Thus it came about that my work for the County Badge Committee ground slowly to a complete halt. In three years my wife and I left Aberdovey together only on one occasion — for a ten-day holiday which was woven round a number of speaking engagements. One became more and more conscious of being cut off from the normal activities of the world and, I have no doubt, inspiration and zest must have declined as staleness set in.

After the passing of the Education Act in 1944, my thoughts

turned with increasing frequency to the enormous possibilities that were to be opened up in the public sector of the education service in which I had spent many happy years. The idea began to grow upon me not only that I would benefit from a change but also that the school would undoubtedly profit if I went. In looking for my successor the directors would almost certainly require nautical experience and men with suitable professional qualifications would be most unlikely to accept the system of remote control which had caused me so much anxiety. An occasion for putting things to the issue very soon presented itself.

Officers who lacked competence or liveliness could seriously affect the activities based upon the wharf. The tempo would be slowed up and this would be reflected in the pace and spirit of the course as a whole. But this alone was seldom disastrous. A period in cutters would last only for a few hours and then the boys would come under other influences. The sea cruise, however, was a matter of far graver moment. Bad weather for two or three days could dampen the adour of a first-class watch of boys and if this was coupled with boredom and a lack of concern for their welfare their morale could be seriously impaired. There had been captains who had relieved the tedium of a winter's anchorage by a spell ashore while a boat's crew of boys stood by on a cold, bleak beach awaiting their convenience. Such occasions would from time to time be quoted as the reason for some unfortunate youth's breakdown on the training condition of non-smoking. Those of us who struggled to strengthen the boys' belief in themselves naturally reacted very strongly. The case on which I was to base my final protest was of this general nature. It took on a far more serious complexion because the captain was accompanied on his shore trip by certain of his subordinate officers. The ship which lay at anchor off-shore was for a time grievously undermanned. Had any situation arisen in which it was necessary for her to be got urgently under way there were insufficient adults on board.

Once more I was obliged to notify Laurence Holt of a situation which I found totally indefensible. He visited Aberdovey at once and, I have no doubt, treated the Captain to a memorable rebuke after which he was able to assure me that the man was unlikely to repeat his error. I was no longer prepared to let matters rest in this way. I pointed out that very shortly the Captain, and all the officers serving with him, were likely to have been replaced by new men who would contribute to our problems in new ways — if not by a repetition of the old. It seemed to me unreasonable that we should remain over a period of years still subject to behaviour which was incompatible with the educational ideals we proclaimed to our customers. In any normal situation the teaching staff of a school would expect to be dismissed quite summarily if they disregarded the requirements of safety as well as of educational effectiveness. I returned to the charge: certain key posts should be held by people employed by and owing their first allegiance to the school. Mr. Holt was adamant. That was not an arrangement he was prepared to contemplate. He returned to Liverpool.

I wrote to Laurence Holt arguing that our performance was consistently falling far below the potential. Though he might justify this because of the advantages conferred on his officers, I was obliged to condemn it because of our obligation to the boys. I could well believe that while the Warden was a non-seaman there would be serious difficulties about introducing significant reform and for that reason it was clear to me that I had no alternative but to resign. I proposed therefore to seek another job forthwith.

Laurence Holt's response was characteristic. He summoned me to Liverpool at once. Our discussion proved fruitless. He had no intention of changing his mind on something which to him was inseparable from his concept of the school. My own attitude was equally firm.

I instanced the kind of difficulties that had arisen over the years and pointed out that, deprived of normal authority over the staff, my sole weapons had been tact and persuasion. No doubt it had been salutary for me to undergo such a prolonged test but I concluded that it had lasted long enough. The school was now well established. The war was nearing its end and there would soon be a wide choice of first-class people well suited by character and experience to conduct an Outward Bound School.

Mr. Holt and his loyal colleague, Brian Heathcote, withdrew to discuss my obstinacy. In due course Heathcote returned. There followed a scene which I still find deeply touching.

They had been shocked that I had reacted as I had. This could only be the consequence of excessive strain and anxiety. They had been guilty of leaving me too long alone "to bear the heat and burden" of establishing the school. Patently what I needed was a proper rest. They therefore suggested I should take a sabbatical year. I had frequently asked in the past that I might make a passage or two in one of their ships so as to lessen my ignorance of the conditions for which we were preparing others. This could now be realised. I could go anywhere I chose on the routes they covered. Wherever I went ashore their agents would see to my well-being. On my return I would be refreshed and strengthened—and would see all our problems from a different point of view!

I was obliged to pursue the course of ungraciousness. It was necessary to underline the fact that in the final issue principles are as important to schoolmasters as to shipowners. Heathcote readily understood that having brought myself to the point of protest I could not place myself irretrievably under obligation to Alfred Holt and Company and return twelve months later to renew the battle exactly where we had left it.

In the event of my being unwilling to compromise Laurence Holt was still generous. Accepting that I intended to go they would consider it deplorable if I acted so precipitately as to prejudice my own interests. I could hand over responsibility for the conduct of the school from such date as I thought fit but my salary would be paid and my quarters would continue to be at my disposal until such time as I had secured a job entirely to my liking.

Within weeks Freddie Fuller had taken over full responsibility at Aberdovey and within a month or so I knew my next assignment. Early in 1945 I left to take up a new job in Somerset. For some time my contacts with the school were to be tenuous and intermittent. What I learned, however, filled me with dismay. Not only had I failed to bring about an improvement; things were to get worse before becoming better.

CHAPTER 14

As long as Freddie Fuller was in charge at Aberdovey there was a balance of advantage and disadvantage. For energy and enthusiasm he was unsurpassed and he coupled these qualities with great practical ability, imagination and an irresistible urge to introduce innovations. All this, backed by Bedwell's influence and wider experience, augured well for the future. Unfortunately, Bedwell's contact was sporadic. His interests were widespread and their demands frequently urgent. Denied the intimate and regular involvement of the Director of Training the Chief Executive Officer had to carry the full burden of day-to-day responsibility. In this a young second mate from the Alfred Holt hierarchy was at even greater disadvantage than a schoolmaster.

If Freddie's position was to be strengthened he had to be advanced in rank. Before this could happen he had to log certain periods of "sea-time," which involved leaving the school for substantial periods. Unless he abandoned his professional career altogether it was prudent for him to insist on maintaining his normal progress through the ranks by service at sea. During his absences other officers returned to assume command of the school. My knowledge of what happened during these intervals is gleaned from my own infrequent visits and occasional correspondence. In most cases I knew the men concerned. Estimable as many of them undoubtedly were, either as professional seamen or as instructors in specific practical activities, I doubt if any of them would have thought themselves well equipped to lead an enterprise dedicated to broader educational purposes. That the school survived the next few years without accident or loss of reputation was a tribute to the soundness of Hahn's original conception, and, perhaps, to the routines and practices that had become part of the the tradition of the place. A school, however, needs more than the painstaking observance of established doctrine. A short - term school, in particular, depends enormously upon the renewal of zest and inspiration. With the war over and the immediate task of pre-service training losing its appeal, future recruitment would depend more and more upon the contribution the school could make to the general development of the ordinary citizen. It was in this respect, that it seemed likely to become less and less distinguished.

After an interval of something approaching two years, rumours began to reach me that moves were afoot to establish an educational trust to safeguard the "Outward Bound" idea. Though there had been no reduction in Laurence Holt's personal interest it is possible that in a situation of peacetime economy he found it more difficult to sustain the scale of the concealed subsidy with which Alfred Holt's had supported the school. It was also becoming more necessary to widen the range of recruitment since boys requiring specific "pre-sea" training were now likely to be reduced in number. The scope of the training would obviously have to be widened; this would be easier of attainment if in staffing the school there were to be less dependence upon the secondment of Alfred Holt's own people. Thus the door might be opened for the appointment of a nucleus of permanent staff — not all of whom necessarily would be professional seamen. Much depended upon the successful establishment of a trust capable of influencing Laurence Holt whose fundamental ideas, I gathered, had not undergone much change.

Slowly but surely developments took place which exceeded my most optimistic expectations. In 1946 the Outward Bound Trust came into being. Of the many well-wishers who were involved, one of the most vigorous was G. Spencer Summers, M.P., who had visited the school during my wardenship. I sought an early opportunity to tell him of my experiences and conclusions. He gave me a patient and courteous hearing. Whether he was entirely persuaded to my point of view I do not know. He made it perfectly clear that the Trust was very much a struggling infant and Laurence Holt's influence was still very strong. Any change which went against his wishes, therefore, was unlikely to occur in the near future. Nevertheless, I drew comfort from the fact that henceforward the school's affairs would be watched most closely by men whose primary concern was with broader educational values rather than with training for a single occupation. Though Aberdovey's problems were not to be immediately dissolved, there was now hope that movement would be in the right direction.

It is somewhat ironic that the first benefits from the establishment of the Trust should have been felt elsewhere than at Aberdovey. Around 1950 I had a number of meetings with John Gwynne who had become the executive director of the Trust. A lawyer by profession, John's wartime exploits with special services had been such as to denote courage of the highest order. This he was now dedicating to a job which had completely captured his loyalty and imagination. Before long he had news of an exciting development. A property in the Lake District had been inspected with a view to the opening of a second school — this time with the accent on training in mountainous terrain rather than on the sea. A supporter of the trust was apparently prepared quite anonymously to loan much of the capital needed for purchase. A board of directors had been formed, a warden appointed and rapid progress was being made on all the preliminaries. John conveyed to me an invitation to join the board, which I accepted with gratitude and alacrity.

When I first visited Eskdale I found it an extraordinarily moving experience. The approach to "Gatehouse," previously the home of the Rea family, is impressive enough. One is conscious of the grandeur of the higher fells of the Scafell group and the proximity of vast areas of remote walking country. I was totally unprepared, however, for the view as one passed through the house from the entrance on the north side to the south-facing windows and terrace. A steeply sloping bank smothered in daffodils was bounded on either flank by masses of rhododendron bushes as it descended to a lovely tarn. Beyond the tarn was a view which took me completely off balance. The shapely summit of Harter Fell erupted from a ruggedly impressive skyline. I had not thought that the new school might be even more fortunate in its physical assets and environment than Aberdovey had been.

The house offered enormous advantage over Bryniethyn. Even without the additions which were subsequently to be made, it provided by no means ungenerously for sizeable courses of boys and a reasonable proportion of resident staff. Equally important was the fact that it had an air and an atmosphere. My own experience at Aberdovey had convinced me that the provision of a gracious 'home base' was a vital part of the task. If one were to expose youngsters for prolonged periods to wet, grime, cold and discomfort and to offer no compensations then one would do nothing to enhance sensitivity, to afford a contrast to what for many was a familiar element in their normal lives. The behaviour of young people is enormously influenced by what appears to be the standard acceptable to those around them. At Aberdovey we had always made much of the necessity for a well-ordered routine. Getting out of working clothes for the evening meal seemed as important as being punctual for the morning parade. My biggest regret was that our spartan beginnings had denied us the advantage of well designed furniture and utensils, of a comely as well as a functionally effective headquarters. Eskdale was starting where we had left off.

There were other respects in which I envied Adam Arnold Brown, the warden. An ex-Gordonstoun boy, his army service had given him excellent experience of training men in mountain activities. Though he had serving under him men to whose mountaineering experience and judgment he would, if necessary, defer, his own knowledge was such that he had little difficulty in acting as "primus inter pares." What is more, all of the instructors were appointed to the staff of the school — not visitors seconded from another employer. And, finally, a team of men carefully selected for the job were assisted by the fact that from the beginning they were adequately equipped; they did not have to accumulate essentials as they went along. This is not to say that as the years went by there was not to be steady improvement and elaboration in the light of experience. Those concerned would probably scoff at the notion that they enjoyed generous provision from the start. All things are comparative. In retrospect I suppose one draws particular satisfaction from being in at the beginning of an enterprise. The sense of achievement can be proportionate to the difficulties that have to be overcome. Be that as it may, Eskdale went off to a flying start. Adam Arnold-Brown was fully aware of Hahn's thinking and educational ideals so that the original training scheme followed very closely the pattern of training that had been set by the County Badge. He himself as a Gordonstoun schoolboy had trained for the Moray Badge along similar lines. Once again the fourfold challenge was presented to the boys — a project concerned with the skills necessary to living and moving in mountainous country, athletics, an expedition of some severity, together with observance of training conditions and service to the general community of the school.

There was more, however, to the successful establishment of the second school than a simple imitation of the first. At Aberdovey the fact that one looked two ways — to the sea and to the mountains — was a considerable advantage. The resulting range of activities helped to stave off the possibilities of staleness in training. When the weather was particularly unsuitable for one or other of the items in our programme rapid changes were readily attainable. It soon became obvious that within a course with his principles. Soon I found myself attempting to justify the which inevitably contained a large element of mountain walking and scrambling it would be impossible to improve the boys' performance in skills which called for resilience or acceleration to high degree. Many of the mountaineers regarded the training in athletics which had been inherited from Aberdovey as completely irrelevant and artificial in the Eskdale context. Zimm was loaned for various periods and did much with his special magic to show how the boys could be galvanised into vigorous striving for improvement. Those who saw what he was able to achieve quickly appreciated that athletics was for him merely a tool whereby a boy could be enabled to grow in confidence and determination. Zimm's demonstration of the craft of the educator was so deeply impressive that many of those who were privileged to see him at work sought to use the same activities to the same ends. Few could delude themselves that they could ever approach the apparently effortless mastery of this great teacher. A number undoubtedly reasoned that the same educational ends ought surely to be attainable by means of practices more in keeping with the character of the school. To those who had been associated with the County Badge campaign, and particularly to Hahn, this represented a dangerous heresy. It was to be some years before the logic and good sense of the heretics were to bring about a major change.

There were other respects in which the new school had to forge new patterns. The whole issue of safety was now to present an entirely new set of problems. Aberdovey had been functioning for nearly a decade without a serious accident. There had been a good share of "near-misses" — each of which had resulted in anxious thought about additional precautions. We had certainly had our share of luck, particularly in the early days before we had built up our defences. Obviously the greatest risks for us had been on the water but there at least we had the advantage of an entirely ... mountains had been day's trudge in the the most formidable of the more exacting re was no doubt that l extend over several ns of the year over mountains which were potentially much more dangerous. It would

ERRATUM

Transfer line one page 87 to line one Page 97.

be impossible to resist the inclusion of some basic training in roped rock climbing. Systems had to be evolved whereby with a limited staff this could be undertaken in a way that gave the highest guarantees of care and responsibility.

The tasks facing Adam Arnold-Brown were onerous. In some respects they were more daunting even than the ones I had faced at Aberdovey. The professional seaman generally has the profoundest respect for the sea. It is a vital part of his training that he shall eschew avoidable risk. One could not be entirely sure that similar qualities would be deeply ingrained in all those who turn to the mountains for their satisfactions. People attracted to the staff of the mountain school were likely to be young and adventurous by disposition. Adam had to be sure that they were sensibly prudent and that in seeking a job which would permit them to pursue their own interests they would learn to subordinate themselves to the educational purposes they were to serve — to which mountaineering would be the means but in no sense the end.

A succession of young and often boisterous men had to be persuaded to discipline themselves into attitudes of care and deep-felt responsibility. That this was successfully accomplished is in itself a great tribute to the leadership that Adam was able to exercise. It was all the more remarkable because he was still a very young man. Admirably supported by his wife he established a team which was dedicated in work and congenial in leisure.

There was one marked difference between the launching of Aberdovey and that of Eskdale. My task had been complicated by the character and relationship of the co-founders, Hahn and Holt. Each had the strongest views about the way we should do our work; though completely agreed on general principles they were often in conflict about important details of practice. Since neither was anxious to compromise both resisted developments which might enable decisions to be taken out of their hands. Although from the beginning there was a board of directors for the school one was never conscious of this as a body in which real power was vested. It met rarely, was, on the whole, ill-attended and concerned itself mainly with matters of finance, recruitment and support. The vital issues of educational practice were settled in other places.

From the beginning Eskdale had a board of directors which took its duties with the utmost seriousness. For some years Lord Rea acted as our chairman; his quiet advice, based upon a profound knowledge of people and places in the locality, enabled the school to gain acceptance in the face of some suspicion. He was supported by as vigorous a group of men as one could wish — bringing from a surprising breadth of experience useful knowledge on practically all the matters that came before them for decision. They developed a tremendous loyalty to the school and battled constantly on its behalf. As time passed they were to find themselves championing ideas of change so fundamental as to require consideration by the Outward Bound Trust itself. The nature of the changes they proposed is discussed later. That many of the ideas came to be accepted was due in no small measure to the quality of the directors of the Eskdale school.

CHAPTER 15

Throughout the 'fifties and the early 'sixties there was to be an enormous growth of the Outward Bound idea. In a sense Eskdale had not been the second school to be established. Shortly after the war Gordonstoun had returned to its normal home in Morayshire and a short-term school had soon been opened in close association with Gordonstoun's own seamanship activities. Its development had been handicapped by inadequate resources and as the Outward Bound Trust grew in strength it was probably inevitable that the Morayshire school should come under its mantle. John Gwynne had been succeeded as Executive Director of the Trust first by Colonel P. D. Maud and subsequently by Eddie Dawson. He had also been joined by another senior officer, Val Lunnon, who became responsible for appeals for support. Over the years Lunnon obtained a remarkable response and as a consequence the Trust was in a position to undertake capital development on an increasing scale. A simple formal relationship was established between the Trust and the schools. The Trust came to be regarded as a parent body responsible for capital expenditure, in whom all properties were vested and with whom finally lay responsibility for broad issues of policy. Each school was registered as a limited liability company and, under its board, was responsible for meeting normal running costs from fee income. In order that subscribers to the Trust could be assured that their gifts would be used, as far as possible, exclusively for development, it was thought important that the schools should not only meet their own running costs but also contribute to such expenditure as the Trust incurred in general publicity or in other ways that might be regarded as a service to the schools themselves.

Since the Eskdale school was the first to be established entirely under the umbrella of the Trust these relationships began to emerge as soon as the school had become economically secure. Before long Aberdovey and Moray fell into a similar pattern.

It was natural that when there were three schools for boys in vigorous operation, complaints began to arise that no provision had been made for girls. While at Aberdovey I had in fact twice arranged rather limited courses for girls. Both were organised in conjunction with the Sea Ranger branch of the Girl Guides Association. In a sense therefore they appealed to girls who had selected themselves by reason of their special interest. They had already attained a high degree of proficiency in many of the skills they were to practise with us and we had little to give them beyond the use of expensive equipment, accommodation and instruction by our expert staff.

The seamen viewed the whole undertaking as amusing or irresponsible. The captain refused to take the girls to sea on the grounds that they would be incapable of handling sail and in indifferent weather would constitute a serious liability. The seamanship instructors maintained that the girls would be unable to handle our heavy cutters in anything but the best of conditions in the estuary.

The girls caused a lot of words to be swallowed. Whatever they lacked in physical robustness they more than made up for in previously gained knowledge and skill as well as in zest and indomitable spirit. After seeing their boatwork in the river the captain grudgingly agreed that, weather permitting, he would give them a full day at sea in the ketch. He returned enthusiastic about their performance, which had surpassed that of any average watch of boys. I had long been conscious that it ought to be possible to offer a form of training to girls which would be acceptable to some and which might be of real benefit to many. For this to be done as a regular feature of a school operating all through the year it would be necessary to submit the general form of the courses offered to boys to critical examination. Though certain general principles might be common to both, I thought some modifications would be necessary.

During the early 'fifties occasional courses for girls were organised at Eskdale. Once again it was shown that the girls' response to demanding situations could be most impressive. Some of the toughest and most sceptical of the climbing instructors were surprised that at the adolescent stage the greater physical maturity, sensitivity and physical co-ordination of the girls gave them in certain circumstances a considerable advantage over the majority of boys of the same age. Those who saw the experimental girls' courses generally voted them a great success. For some years the Trust met the demand for more by working in close partnership with the Central Council for Physical Recreation and using their excellent centre at Bisham Abbey as well as by planning occasional courses at one or other of the boys' schools. This did not satisfy the feminists, who felt that nothing short of equal opportunity was good enough.

The Trust could be forgiven for proceeding cautiously. The capital needed to establish a new school and subsidise its operation until full recruitment was assured became increasingly formidable as costs rose throughout the 'fifties. Senior management in industry had come to regard the cost of boys' courses as a sound investment in training, but there were few who felt that a girl's industrial life and role were such as to promise a comparable return for a similar investment. Thus it came about that the fifth school to be established (at Holne Park in Devon) was to be used partly for girls' courses and partly for boys. Before this happened a second mountain school had been set up on the shore of Ullswater. From the beginning this school worked in close partnership with Eskdale, each gaining from the exchange of experience and each experimenting and pioneering new approaches and methods according to the expert knowledge of the changing staffs.

The tale of expansion in this country was completed when in the early 'sixties the girls at last acquired a school exclusively for themselves. "Rhowniar," an attractive house only four miles from Aberdovey, was taken over and greatly expanded by the addition of well-planned extensions. It had perhaps been worth waiting to gain a base with such obvious advantages.

Devon could now be devoted solely to boys' courses. In roughly a decade and a half from the foundation of the Trust the British establishment had been expanded from one school to six and the annual capacity from some 1,200 boys to approximately 5,000 boys and nearly 1,000 girls. The officers and active members of the Trust had good reason to congratulate themselves. Though the knighthood conferred on Sir Spencer Summers was for distinguished work in other fields, it might just as appropriately have been in recognition of vigorous and devoted service he had given as Chairman of the Management Committee of the Trust since its inception. Under his guidance the schools in this country had not only increased in number; all had benefited enormously from extensions and improvements. Equipment and methods had been overhauled so that Outward Bound had come to be recognised as commanding a certain authority in the whole business of education through adventure.

The achievement of the Trust extended far beyond the successful operation of six schools in the British Isles. The idea of challenging the young in a variety of outdoor pursuits had gained widespread recognition. In many cases elements of the Outward Bound programme were assimilated into the practice of schools which for good reasons felt unable to adopt the whole. A large number of local education authorities as well as voluntary organisations established their own schools and centres for training in outdoor pursuits in Scotland, the Lake District, Snowdonia and elsewhere. This was all a positive gain and it is no small advantage that there should be a widely different approach, as for instance at Brathay Hall, to broadly similar purposes.

Apart from those who have adopted training in adventurous pursuits without the particular emphasis characteristic of Outward Bound schools there are a number of open imitators. It is many years since the British Army established it own "Army Outward Bound School" for young serving soldiers. And certain Police forces now organise courses for their cadets which they openly describe as "Outward Bound" in character.

Over the years Outward Bound Schools have been set up in Africa (where there are three — all recruiting multi-racially), Malaya, New Zealand, Australia, Germany (a sea school on the Baltic coast and a mountain school in Bavaria), Holland and, more recently, in America.

These developments have put a heavy strain upon the Trust since frequently Wardens and/or chief instructors have been drawn from the staffs of the British schools. Maintaining the quality of work at home in face of a drain of this kind is a matter of serious concern though so far every effort has been made to meet demands.

Extension overseas has not been without some advantages. Some years ago a group of people who were interested in launching the Outward Bound idea in America turned to the Trust in this country for advice. It was agreed to loan Freddie Fuller for consultation and he was flown to Colorado to examine a possible site for a school. He addressed meetings of potential supporters and had the satisfaction of knowing that he had played a significant part in bringing about the establishment of the first American Outward Bound School.

Later he was invited to Washington to outline the principles of Outward Bound training to Mr. Sargent Shriver and many of the administrators of the Peace Corps Volunteers organisaton. These discussions resulted in Freddie being rushed to Puerto Rico where, after a helicopter reconnaissance and visits to many parts of the island, he assisted in choosing the site for an experimental Peace Corps camp at which volunteers, before going overseas, could be put through a course modelled in many respects upon the well-tried Outward Bound pattern. Shortly afterwards his services were again requested so that he might supervise the training on the initial courses of the Peace Corps camp which was established in Puerto Rico in 1963.

One of the Americans loaned to help in launching the new venture was a Mr. Fred Lanoue, from the staff of the Georgia Institute of Technology. Mr. Lanoue had for many years been teaching a remarkable technique of survival in deep water which he called "drown-proofing." At its simplest this consisted of learning to relax in the water, utilising the buoyancy of the body. As long as a quantity of air is retained in the lungs swimmers can remain just below the surface, exerting only such minimal energy as is necessary to raise the body at appropriate intervals for an exchange of air. When the preliminary techniques are mastered learners can be taught to propel themselves in a leisurely manner and in such a way that they can progress for very long distances without fatigue. Apparently these methods were taught at Puerto Rico and quite elderly volunteers who had previously been non-swimmers were able to pass the stipulated tests of remaining afloat in deep water for not less than an hour and travelling for not less than a mile.

Inevitably Freddie himself had to sample this experience. Although previously he had claimed to be only a very moderate swimmer he returned to this country fired with missionary zeal. He had himself become a most effective performer and is convinced that "drown-proofing" represents a life-saving technique of very great potential. Certainly it has been introduced into the programme at Aberdovey with astonishing results and Freddie himself has been responsible for its being adopted increasingly in other areas of this country.

It was not only in the training of Peace Corps Volunteers, however, that Outward Bound played its part in America. Shortly schools catering for young people on the same lines as in this country had been founded in Colorado, Minnesota and Maine, and once again experienced British instructors played an important part in passing on the benefits of their experience.

What had started in 1941 as a very limited demonstration had, by 1963, established a footing in four continents and had exerted an influence upon the practice of very great numbers of schools and organisations in no way connected with the Outward Bound Trust. This must be attributed entirely to the soundness of Hahn's original conviction; it is not to say that there had been no growth or even departure from the original design. Fortunately there has been constant evidence of such reappraisal and adjustment as is essential to continued vitality and relevance to social need. In following chapters I hope to touch upon the most significant changes that have in fact taken place, and one of these represents the second bonus from Freddie Fuller's experience in Puerto Rico. None of these later developments however detracts in any way from the importance of the original inspiration and conception.

CHAPTER 16

Having established Eskdale as a going concern Adam Arnold-Brown considered that he should widen his own experience. Before settling the final form of his career in education he felt, I am sure rightly, that he should practise the art of the schoolmaster in more orthodox fields. There followed a brief spell when Eskdale was under the wardenship of Eric Shipton. It is impossible to imagine a more authoritative head of a school dedicated to training in mountaineering and those who were closely associated with him cannot fail to have been greatly influenced. It is important to remember however that Outward Bound Schools exist not to train for mountaineering or for careers at sea. Their object is the strengthening of the individual through contact with the forces of nature. Hence it is vital that those responsible for the conduct of the schools should be more concerned with ends than with means — with people than with techniques. When Shipton decided to return to fields of activity in which his real genius had so often been displayed he was succeeded by John Lagoe, the chief instructor.

John was an educator by profession. As a young graduate he had had a short experience in a secondary modern school before joining the Eskdale staff in order to satisfy his love of the mountains. There his steadiness and sturdy good sense had led to his promotion to Chief Instructor and finally to his becoming warden while still in his twenties. It was not long before one became aware of the exercise of a vigorously critical mind on the work of the school.

Because of my own past experience and professional interests Wardens frequently discussed with me the detailed practical problems of doing the job. Whenever I had disagreed with Adam it had tended to be over the treatment of one of the unfortunates of society who had failed to come up to some of the requirements of the course. Adam had been lucky in his family and educational background and found it difficult to understand, still less sympathise with, the inveterate sinners and blunderers. With John Lagoe one dealt with a totally different phenomenon. His concern for justice and his regard for the youngsters caused him to call into question any procedure which seemed incompatible retention of practices which had previously enjoyed an unchallenged place in the Outward Bound concept and programme. It was salutory that these should be submitted to rigorous re-examination by a man who combined Yorkshire pertinacity with unusual courage and integrity — the full strength of which was at first unsuspected because they were combined with great restraint and quietness of manner.

Although he was a non-smoker John constantly called our attention to the difference in degree of the demands made by our training conditions. Throughout his course each boy was expected to deny himself smoking and alcohol. If he yielded to temptation he was expected to say so. Even if he distinguished himself in all other aspects of the training he could not qualify for the Outward Bound Badge until he could make the necessary declaration that he had fulfilled this particular condition for the requisite twenty-six days. This had always borne much more heavily on some than on others. Many youngsters were already confirmed and heavy smokers before attending the schools. We had long been conscious that a small minority had broken their undertakings and accepted their badges because they were prepared to lie quite barefacedly about it.

It would have been easy to avoid an irksome difficulty by conceding that in some cases it represented a considerable triumph if a boy succeeded merely in reducing his smoking. One could have devised a set of rules whereby limited smoking might have been permitted in specified places and at limited times. There were however good grounds for approaching such a solution with real misgiving. It was always depressing to see a teenager already deeply enslaved to the smoking habit. One might think that by enabling any substantial proportion of such boys to break free — even if only for the duration of the course — one was conferring a notable benefit. One of the objects of the entire exercise was to give the boys confidence in themselves — which should, of course, include convincing them of their capacity to accept the burden of self-discipline. Furthermore, one would do nothing to eliminate dishonesty simply by removing the temptations to practise deceit.

In the 1940's excessive smoking represented no more than a surrender to habit-forming indulgence and, perhaps, an extravagance. It has now become probable that it also involves an indefensible health hazard. Since the publication of recent reports the case for the relaxation of Outward Bound conditions would seem to be weaker than before. This is not to say that it was not right that the whole thing should be questioned and carefully debated. One of the consequences of such discussion has been the more open-minded and experimental approach to this problem in the "Senior" courses which were pioneered at Eskdale.

On the cessation of National Service many firms asked for the admission to the courses of young men who had passed the normal upper age limit of 19 years. There were good arguments for not taking young men on to courses primarily designed for adolescents. They could easily deny opportunities to those younger than themselves to exercise responsibility and leadership among their peers. It was decided to offer a limited number of courses specifically for "Seniors"—that is young men roughly between the ages of 20 and 25. In many cases these men have been offered the choice of outright acceptance of the normal training conditions or an undertaking of severe limitation of smoking and drinking. To their credit the majority have elected to demand of themselves conditions no less severe than those imposed upon the younger trainees.

In pioneering the work with older people John Lagoe was able to devise programmes that contained rather more stimulus to careful thought about social, political, economic, and industrial problems. There had always been a great eagerness to encourage the youngsters to discuss and think out the problems which affected their everyday lives, not excluding their own religious beliefs. John's own interests in this field enabled him to make an important contribution to evolving a supplement to the physical activities.

The second respect in which John Lagoe attacked one of the "sacred cows" of the original badge programme was when he denounced the athletic tests as an irrelevant part of a course centred upon mountaineering techniques. In this he shared and acted as mouthpiece for the views of his young colleagues. One of these was responsible for suggesting an interesting alternative which John pressed upon us all with the utmost vigour. In the later 'fifties considerable publicity had been given to "circuit-training." A book on this subject by R. E. Morgan and G. T. Adamson described what had been done at Leeds University to enable undergraduates to enhance and maintain fitness by short visits to a gym specially equipped to enable them individually in a relatively short time to go through a prescribed number of exercises involving simple apparatus. The exercises consisted mainly of lifting and heaving, and performance could be measured and progress noted either by timing each complete circuit or by the inclusion within the individual assignment of a more exacting requirement as strength mounted.

The Eskdale team had had a simple circuit constructed out of doors and had satisfied themselves that individual assignments could be evolved and targets of progress agreed in such a way as to provide a completely satisfactory substitute for tests in javelin throwing, sprinting, jumping and the like. John suggested that the longer distance runs should be replaced by cross-country courses on the fells and that the less "relevant" sprints, jumps and throws should be abandoned in favour of the circuit exercises. Such a programme of training was likely to produce forms of fitness and stamina needed for successful work in the hills which in turn would contribute to progress towards the circuit targets of performance.

All this was entirely sound. There was no doubt that boys' performances in sprinting and jumping had frequently deteriorated rather than improved as a consequence of the slow rhythmic style they had been encouraged to adopt for mountain walking. Nevertheless, if accepted, this meant a further erosion of the original badge scheme. I still cherished the hope that the day might yet come when the badge idea might become accepted more widely and had serious reservations about the abandonment of any important part of the scheme so far practised in Outward Bound Schools. The rest of the Directors were less conservative. They were convinced by demonstrations of what could be done by means of circuit training and a change in the physical tests for the Badge was accepted on an experimental basis at Eskdale. I had no doubt about the outcome of this "experiment." In education it nearly always happens that so-called experiments are conducted by teachers who are zealots and probably amongst the ablest of their profession. The prospects of failure therefore are fairly slight! Certainly it was so in this case. From time to time the circuit apparatus has been revised and improved but it now provides a well-established part of the training programme not only at Eskdale but also in other Outward Bound Schools which have recognised that it contributes to a gain in strength and fitness in a way that convinces the boys of its effectiveness.

After such substantial victories over the die-hards, I had

thought John would have been content to rest on his laurels. Soon, however, he was casting doubts not merely upon individual elements in the original badge scheme but also upon the case for retaining any badge at all as an incentive to hard training. We argued for months in private and in front of the whole board of directors. I brought out all the arguments about the way in which insistence upon all-round achievement enabled a boy to overcome his lack of confidence in himself by defeating his own defeatism. I instanced case after case in which the thing had patently worked in a quite significant way.

There was one devastating reply to all this. As long as we adhered to our rigid standards over half the boys were going away with no more than the Membership Badge. It was possible to argue that the Merit Badge which was awarded to those who reached all of the standards in all activities was, as its name implied, a reward for effort and achievement much above the average. Nevertheless it was maintained that alongside this the Membership Badge could not fail to be regarded as a sort of consolation prize. When I argued that boys could in fact go back to their homes and complete the tests thus qualifying either for a Merit or Honours Badge the miserable numbers of those who actually did so were quoted against me. Most telling of all, course after course revealed that some of those who had no hope at all of earning a Merit Badge were by any sane judgment harder triers and better chaps altogether than many to whom success came quite easily. There was no point in denying this. It had always been true. The only justification for maintaining an arrangement which was so palpably unfair was that the original object had been to bring about a more widespread acceptance of the County Badge idea. It seemed to me that instead of impairing or destroying the original concept we ought to be making all possible endeavours to enable more and more of the boys to bring their training to a successful conclusion in their home areas. In various places Outward Bound old boys and supporters had been forming local associations. If these could be galvanised into organising "follow-on" work we could hope that boys would be encouraged and assisted to extend their training, and also that some of the more valuable elements of Outward Bound training might be accepted into more general practice.

It was true that by far the greater number who failed to gain more than a Membership Badge were impeded simply by difficulties in the physical tests. That a boy who had done splendidly in all other aspects of a widely demanding course should be denied the crown of achievement by falling short of, say, the high jump requirement by no more than an inch or so was utterly galling. In a longer course or, better still, in his own school or youth organisation it would almost certainly have proved possible to urge, wheedle and coax him past all obstacles — for none of the standards were beyond the ultimate reach of normal youngsters — but there was no point in denying that once removed from the pressing influence of an Outward Bound School few youngsters would receive the day-to-day encouragement needed for absolute all-round victory.

In 1954 the Outward Bound Trust organised a conference at Ashorne Hill at which Wardens, Directors of Schools, sponsors and others took careful stock of current practice. Later, a group of those most involved in the controversy about the badge scheme met to argue it out.

It soon became clear that Sir Spencer Summers had become convinced that some concession had to be made to the objectors. He suggested a compromise which won a great deal of support from all but the out-and-out die-hards — which included Freddie Fuller and myself. This was that there should continue to be three graded badges, by this time known as Membership, Merit and Honours. To qualify for each of these boys would, as previously, be required to reach appropriate standards in a project of "technical" training, an expedition, and service to the community as well as to observe the stipulated training conditions of the schools. In future, however, attainment in physical tests was to be indicated by a defined "rim" to the badge, the colour of which would indicate his level of performance. I must confess that my own objection to this solution was based not only upon the "demotion" of the physical tests as one of the important areas of endeavour but, perhaps even more, upon the complicated system of badges which then had to be evolved; for each of the graded badges there was a possibility of differing rims. The previous system had been criticised on the grounds that it was complicated. Now it was to become even more so. Nevertheless a move was promised in what the majority thought to be the right direction and when, to my astonishment, Hahn gave it his support the compromise was generally welcomed.

None of this completely satisfied the views of John Lagoe and his team of instructors. They had no nostalgia for the ideas that had possessed us in 1941. Their concern was solely for the facts of the late 'fifties. It was their conviction that there was something very much more compelling and challenging in the real situations into which they were placing boys in the mountains than in any predetermined and, by comparison, rather artificial requirements. They continued to contrast the incentives to personal progress provided by the badge scheme with the incentives to greater effort arising out of patrol competitions and the total attitude towards fitness for community service with which the staff constantly sought to inspire the school as a whole.

I cannot ever recall being in a position in which I felt more ill at ease. Since I had left Aberdovey in 1945 I had been mainly employed in inspecting educational establishments. I had seen much which by its sheer excellence had forced me to a less dogmatic and infinitely more humble approach to educational theories; I had also realised that true education is a process of the greatest subtlety which depends upon sympathetic communication and the "striking of sparks." Some of the masters of the art pursue methods which are highly unorthodox and no-one achieves significant success merely by aping others and blindly accepting any prescription of method or procedure. Faced by sincere men whose influence on boys was obviously profound it went much against my conscience to argue that they should accept directives about the methods they should employ. Yet it was hard also to acknowledge finally that the purpose of the campaign started nearly twenty years earlier should now formally be abandoned.

At Eskdale mine was a small and isolated voice in this matter. After prolonged trial of the revised badge system the Board concluded that the advice offered by their young and enlightened Warden must be supported. They made representations to the Management Committee of the Trust that the time had come for a further overhaul of certain fundamentals of the Outward Bound Badge system. There followed a memorable week-end when representatives of all the schools, together with officers of the Trust, spent a working week-end as guests of Sir Spencer and Lady Summers. Hahn was staying nearby and joined us for the majority of our sessions. It must have been a formidable experience for John Lagoe to be opposed to the combined conservative fervour of Hahn, Freddie Fuller and myself. It did not seem possible that he could carry the day. Certainly the occasion was one which made heavy demands upon Sir Spencer's gifts as a fair minded and conciliatory chairman. I had noticed on previous occasions his genius for extracting the elements on which it might be possible to base the beginnings of compromise but I doubted if this was an occasion on which he could expect any notable success. I was wrong. Thanks to his skill, John Lagoe's indomitable courage and the exhibition of what was, I thought, a new and unexpected tendency towards mellowing on Hahn's part, there was real and welcome progress in our thinking on this vexed business.

At the conclusion of the week-end a summary of conclusions was drawn up which represented a pronounced move in John's direction. Since we had not felt able to go as far as he felt necessary he drew up a "minority" report in which he set out the reasons for his dissatisfaction. Both reports were in due course presented to the Management Committee of the Trust with a result which I personally had not foreseen. It was the Minority Report which commended itself to them so that John Lagoe had won his victory against formidable odds. Henceforward there was to be one badge only for all who completed an Outward Bound course without discredit.

In one respect alone did the Management Committee depart from what John had recommended. They agreed that there might occasionally be boys whose attitude to the course and to their fellows was such as to warrant special distinction. Thus was originated the idea of the "Warden's Badge" which might be awarded to boys not because of outstanding performance — practical or intellectual — but for effort and helpfulness markedly beyond reasonable expectation.

These discussions were taking place at a time when the Duke of Edinburgh had given his support and authority for an Award Scheme which was to gain more general acceptance than could have been expected for any proposal with less eminent sponsorship. The case for regarding Outward Bound schools as demonstrations of any single narrowly particular mechanism of education had thus been totally undermined.

On balance I have no doubt that the abandonment of the scheme of graded badges was a move in the right direction. Used by people who were convinced of its virtues the old system had achieved remarkable results. Certainly it had helped to stir the apathetic and those who lacked faith in their own potential. It would be idle however to pretend that similar results could be obtained in no other way. In education it is desirable that men should be free to adopt methods which best accord with their own sense of purpose. What is indefensible is that they should be required to adhere to practices which conflict with what they conceive to be their duty to the young.

In due course John Lagoe, in turn, decided that he had made his personal contribution and ought to move on. There are few men — and I have yet to refer again to a notable exeception — who can continue beyond their middle years and still keep up the pressure necessary for such an exacting task as leading an Outward Bound community. No doubt John was extremely wise to consider re-finding his place in the outside world but it was a cause of great regret that he should have been attracted into industry rather than into the normal educational agencies. Possibly the emergence of a new pattern of industrial training will give scope to his qualities as an innovator. In any case it was clear that we would be lucky to discover a successor of comparable calibre.

CHAPTER 17

In appointing John Lagoe's successor the Directors of Eskdale once again chose a man who was a schoolmaster by profession. Tom Price was older than John and had already established himself as a successful teacher. His slight build and diffident manner gave no indication of his inner toughness and physical stamina. He had taken part in expeditions to South Georgia and Lapland and had climbed regularly for most of his life. His wartime service had been in the Royal Navy and following this he had for many years served as bowman and signalman of the Workington Lifeboat.

No one could have been better fitted to continue the enlightened development of the school. Under his influence the activities in the mountains took on fresh edge and yet, no doubt because of his wide experience and maturity of judgment, there was no tendency towards foolhardiness or excess. We were lucky that once again the school was being led by a man of conscience, acutely sensitive to the needs of individual boys and capable of viewing day to day practice in the light of an intelligent appraisal of ultimate purpose.

Before returning to the affairs of my first love — Aberdovey — I should at least pay my respects to the other schools. My knowledge of them is limited, except in the case of Ullswater to the board of which I was elected in 1964.

One of the problems which has faced the Trust has been that of ensuring recruitment to the schools throughout the year. The peak demand for places falls upon the summer months. To be sure of a boy's acceptance in July or August one needs to book months — if not years — ahead. But there are nearly always vacancies in January and February. This is easy to understand but it is unfortunate. In some respects the winter courses can be even more effective — if not obviously more enjoyable — than the summer ones. One is more likely to get good — if rather cold — sailing, or the chance of training in snow and ice climbing, not to mention ski-ing! From the financial point of view the fees can only be held down if the constant overhead costs of the schools can be matched by full income from each course.

It was a very great temptation for the newer schools which

had not yet built up firm support for all seasons of the year to consider any possibilities of augmenting their income. Ullswater and Moray had forged close relationships with a number of Local Education Authorities which showed interest in the idea of sponsoring the attendance of secondary modern school pupils. In the early fifties there were undoubtedly numbers of schools which were "secondary" only in name. It was to require years of capital building and recruitment of specialist staff before many of these schools could really claim to be offering anything significantly different from what had been available before the passing of the 1944 Act. Some Authorities, anxiously aware of these facts and concerned about their inability to effect any rapid change, envisaged the Outward Bound courses as a compensation and a stimulus to children who in certain other respects were doomed to a degree of deprivation.

There were obvious objections to accepting children aged 13 or 14 on courses generally designed for young men aged up to 19. The idea was entertained of running a number of courses exclusively for the younger ones, and in the development of this work Ullswater played a leading role.

In the "standard" courses youngsters were exposed to situations in which their physical resources, courage and judgment were put under some strain. A good deal of experience had been gained about the degrees of strain that were effective and reasonable. No one could be sure whether by a simple graduation of the demands made upon them younger boys would respond in the same way. Nor could one be sure whether it was wise to encourage boys in the earlier stages of adolescence to undertake exploits which might bring them too close to the limits of their endurance. Common prudence would indicate the need for closer supervision, which in itself might rob some of the activities of much of their effectiveness in the development of character.

Whatever the educational arguments for caution, the financial inducements to undertake experiments were irresistible and occasional Junior courses are now organised at most of the schools. Certainly they have caused astonishment to many of the staffs of the schools who were unprepared for the difference in the general attitudes and behaviour of boys only, on average, two years younger than those on the normal courses. Tom Price sums up the distinction:

"Though the junior boys spent a considerable part of their

time being boys in an exasperating fashion and occasionally even to the dilapidation of the School property, we enjoyed having them, admired many of them for their resilience and gaiety, and perhaps envied them for the very thing we were trying to wean them away from, their capacity to live only in the moment."

Courses for a younger age group have assisted the Trust at a difficult period of development and have contributed to the decisions of an increasing number of Local Education Authorities to establish their own centres for training in adventurous outdoor pursuits. This has resulted in a widening of opportunity. As other agencies establish centres for schoolchildren however, the case for Outward Bound Schools continuing to cater for them will progressively be weakened and it is hoped that there will be sufficient demand to justify concentration upon the older adolescents with whom the schools are probably more convincingly successful.

There is one other respect in which I have been impressed by Ullswater's special contribution. Throughout the time I have known the school the Warden has been Squadron-Leader Lester Davies. As an ex-regular officer it is not surprising that he has a strong interest in organisation and equipment. Ullswater was the first school to have a hall designed down to the last detail for efficiency as a lecture centre. Provision was made from the beginning for the use of modern audio-visual aids. This was also the first school to employ a jet-powered boat as a tender for canoeing. Because of its shallow draft, this craft can operate as close escorts for canoeists both in the deep water lakes and in the treacherous fast running rivers which connect them.

Latterly Ullswater has become what must surely be the first school in the world to equip its parties with the latest walkie-talkie apparatus. Expedition parties can establish contact with the school in case of need and the school can play a more effective part in mountain rescue operations in which the aid of Outward Bound Schools is frequently enlisted. Nothing elicits a more powerful response from young people than the genuine need for their services but one regrets the carelessness and lack of knowledge which leads so many to risk the lives of others as well as their own by foolhardy enterprises in the mountains. Many already owe their survival to the rescue services in which the schools have played a particularly active part.

Of the remaining British schools I can say little from first hand experience, having paid only short visits to Holne Park in Devon, Moray and Rhowniar. The Devon school has exploited its local terrain by developing most ambitious schemes of cliff rescue and off-shore canoeing. Moray until recently had the distinction of being the only one of the schools to maintain a sizeable sea-going craft. After using the old Prince Louis for some time the school acquired a handsome and much larger topsail schooner which regularly cruised out to the Orkneys and Hebrides and around the north of Scotland. It is possible that the larger size of the ship and the generally rather longer cruises enabled the boys to gain more from the experience than was usually possible in the case of the smaller craft operating within the more restricting circumstances of Cardigan Bay in war-time. Nevertheless after protracted experience and debate even in this school the use of a sea going schooner was abandoned in 1966 and replaced — as at Aberdovey — by more ambitious exercises in cutters escorted by a powered lifeboat.

In addition the Moray School has the challenge of expeditions across the Cairngorms — certainly the most formidable terrain used by any of the British schools. It has been possible for ambitious expeditions to be undertaken in the course of which boys have completed one "leg" of the journey in cutters, one by canoe and one on foot over exceptionally arduous country.

I should greatly regret it if the scanty reference to the schools of which I have little direct knowledge were thought to reveal partisanship or lack of regard for their work. It would be impertinent for me to attempt to describe their growth and activities simply from knowledge which has been gained mainly at second hand. They in their turn will surely throw up their own historians.

CHAPTER 18

As I recorded earlier, from the time I left Aberdovey until the Trust had become sufficiently established to assume full responsibility there was a period during which purely make-shift arrangements were made for the day-to-day control of the school. During this time Freddie Fuller went back to sea, first as a 1st mate and finally in command. All this having been accomplished, the time came when the Trust were able to offer him a permanent appointment as Warden. Since that date in 1952 the development of the school has in many respects reflected the extraordinary range of his personal interests and enthusiasms.

From the earliest days it was obvious that Freddie felt a need to widen the scope of the school's activities. While the war was still in progress he made out a powerful case for pig-keeping as an educational side-line and a useful act of self-interest on the part of the school. He enlisted the co-operation of a large number of boys and concrete piggeries began to spring up in unexpected places.

Later, Freddie conceived the idea that homing pigeons could afford a pleasant interest for the boys as well as a means of communication between the ships and expedition parties and the school itself. This had a great deal to commend it. Apparently, however, for such a venture to be successful the pigeons had to be of an expensive highly trained strain which required to be tended with special care. If allowed to stray from their home loft or to interbreed with untrained pigeons their homing instincts would be impaired. Thus when he faced the necessity to return for another spell at sea Freddie meticulously instructed one of the officers on the responsibilities that were to be entrusted to him.

Alas, on his return the consequences of neglect were all too obvious. There was a vastly increased colony of pigeons, all of whom showed homing propensities which were minimal. In a rage at the loss of a costly amenity Freddie informed the man who had failed him that he would be required to make amends for his misdemeanour. The birds had become quite useless and would have to be destroyed. This would be done by wringing all their necks that very night. The massacre could only be perpetrated in the dark hours when all the boys would be asleep. Stealthily Freddie entered the loft, captured the pigeons one by one and passed them to the luckless officer to whom was entrusted the task of wringing their necks and placing them in a large sack. From time to time Freddie inquired whether the gruesome work was being prosecuted with proper effect and was assured that a sound job was being done. It took hours before the two men had completed their unenviable task and could retire to their beds.

The following morning Freddie gave thought to the disposal of the carcasses. Having decided upon a suitable spot for the burial he accompanied the young officer to the place where the sack lay concealed in the undergrowth. As they prepared to move it Freddie thought he detected a slight movement. The thought crossed his mind that one of the pigeons had not been effectively despatched. He untied the mouth of the sack and out flew a swarm of angry birds! I have never discovered how finally they were disposed of.

Freddie was undeterred by minor setbacks of this kind. Once he was permanently established as Warden he set himself to overhaul and enlarge the training possibilities of the school and every aspect of its organisation. One of the first things requiring attention was the accommodation. The school had suffered from the expansion into widely scattered premises. It was not long before the steeply sloping walled garden immediately above Bryneithyn had been levelled into terraces and a series of huts had been concentrated there, each providing adequate accommodation for a complete watch. In due course the wooden huts were replaced by more permanent buildings. Next Freddie conducted a vigorous campaign for donations for the erection of a school chapel and before long a delightful building had been placed in a commanding but isolated part of the grounds. Later a new sick-bay was provided in a building which also housed women members of staff and a school shop. The construction of a new hall together with well-appointed single rooms for unmarried and temporary male staff substantially completed a series of measures to turn the school buildings into an efficient, conveniently concentrated whole. Further refinements may follow, but there is now an impression of good order and permanence about the place. This has not been achieved by any serious diminution of the charm of the grounds. On the contrary, Barbara Fuller, Freddie's wife, has devoted herself not only to the provision of warm and generous hospitality indoors but to a ceaseless care for the loveliness of the gardens.

One further structural feat calls for special mention. When he returned from Puerto Rico Freddie was possessed with the idea of introducing "drown-proofing" to this country and especially to his own school. Throughout the summer he was able to teach a large number of boys in the waters of the estuary. This was far from ideal from an instructional point of view and it was obvious that with the onset of cold weather there would be a long "off-season." This was a notion that Freddie found unacceptable and, as usual, he set himself to the task of raising such capital as would be necessary to provide the basic material for a swimming bath. It could not have been fortuitous that the contractors who were excavating for the foundations of the new hall were inveigled into employing their machinery on digging out the site of the new bath. Nor could it have been pure luck that a new heating plant recently installed for the boys' showers and wash places had such spare capacity as would permit it to be used for the heating of the bath — which was to be sited immediately alongside. By the purchase of suitable prefabricated materials and the employment of voluntary labour there came into being in unbelievably rapid time a heated swimming pool approximately 34ft. by 17ft. and 6ft. in depth *all over*. Patently this was a bath designed for a specific purpose!

It has now been in use for some years, during which time thousands of youngsters have been enabled to master the drown-proofing technique. On each course a number "join the Seal Club" — that is, demonstrate their capacity to stay afloat for not less than six hours. Several, in fact, insist on "bobbing" for upwards of twelve hours and then have to be persuaded that any longer demonstration would merely cause inconvenience all round. The pool has also enabled the school to offer excellent training in under-water swimming, canoe rolling and other exciting techniques.

"Drown-proofing" was only one of the additions that Freddie had made at Aberdovey. He had established a fruitful relationship with local officers of the Forestry Commission; as a result they set aside timber and taught successive parties of boys the techniques of log-cabin construction. In a relatively short time the range of the expeditions had been considerably extended. Parties using the log huts as transit camps did some voluntary work in the forests and came to a greater understanding of the work of the foresters and of the need for care in forested areas. Henceforward parties passing through the attractive forests to the north of Aberdovey were sure of a cordial welcome.

Another form of training which was to become a strongly developed aspect of the school's life was fire-fighting. The school was entrusted with a small fire tender and successive groups of boys were initiated into its efficient operation.

Two other new activities were to be introduced into the land-based side of the school's programme. First Freddie's own love of riding and of animals led him to introduce horsemanship. When the small farm above Bryneithyn fell vacant it was converted into a base for the riders and stables for some fourteen horses. The culmination of this form of training took the form of attractive treks over the nearby hills. As an alternative boys could opt for climbing. After preliminary training on the limited cliffs and faces in the neighbourhood they could look forward to lightweight camping and more challenging movement across country in Snowdonia.

Re-appraisal was also taking place regarding the activities on the water. When Gordonstoun returned to its home in Scotland the Prince Louis left Aberdovey. The life of the Garibaldi was limited and she was soon replaced by a handsome ketch, the Warspite, which was loaned by the Marine Society. Previously a private yacht, she was not really large enough or rugged enough for the heavy duty of all-the-year-round sailing in Cardigan Bay. In due course she too was replaced by a converted motor fishing vessel. Here if anywhere was the ideal craft for the job. Shallow in draught, amply powered and handy in the approaches to the difficult harbours of the bay, she offered freedom of movement and manoeuvre superior to that of any of her predecessors. Nevertheless, she too in turn was to be abandoned.

The maintenance of any sailing craft capable of operating in all weathers with the safety margins appropriate to a training establishment is bound to involve heavy expense. Furthermore, it would be indefensible to allow any vessel to cruise without such strength of professional crew as would enable them to operate the ship even if all the trainees were totally incapacitated by sickness. The burden involved could only be justified if it could be established beyond all doubt that the training advantages were such as could be achieved in no other way. As I have indicated earlier, this was a matter on which I had grave personal doubts. Only a professional seaman could investigate the possible alternatives.

One of the things which changed the conception of what was feasible on the water was the acquisition of a R.N.L.I. lifeboat. With this as tender the heavier cutters could venture out to sea and make passages along the coast. The school was in due course entrusted with a rubber Zodiac R.N.L.I. rescue boat which, because of its high speed and shallow draught, was ideal for a safety boat in the river. It became possible for the lifeboat to escort the cutters without leaving the dinghies and canoes devoid of protective cover. Thus a new pattern of activity on the water began to emerge.

When I last visited the school several cutters were sailing south to Newquay equipped with lightweight camping gear and full rations, completely prepared to remain away for several days on an adventurous expedition. In the lower part of the estuary boys were sailing dinghies without officers, while miles up river twelve boys in single canoes were returning from an expedition in the hills to the south.

Aberdovey had always shown a particular interest in life-saving techniques and had constantly strived to relate these to the idea of service. From the earliest days there had been practice with rocket apparatus and for a time efforts had been made to assist in the manning of the coastguard station. None of this however was really very convincing, partly because during the war there was very little shipping in the vicinity and civilian activities on the water were at a very low ebb.

The situation today is entirely different. Equipped with the high-speed Zodiac rescue boat and the latest breathing apparatus, the school can play a particularly effective part in rescue service in an estuary where the unwary can all too easily find themselves in serious danger. Thus all the boys have an opportunity to prepare themselves for practical aid to their fellows on the water, in fire-fighting or in mountain search and rescue parties.

Two benefits derived from Freddie's experience with the Peace Corps Volunteers in Puerto Rico. The first was drown-proofing, which is gaining some acceptance in this country. The second was the basis of a valuable development which took place in the summer of 1967. The slums of Puerto Rico presented a challenge to the Peace Corps Volunteers at least equal to that they met in the rivers and jungles. Freddie came home convinced that it would be possible to devise a course for young people in an urban setting in which they would be faced with tasks just as demanding as those they had tackled on the sea and the mountains. I must confess the scepticism with which I first reacted to this idea. In the end, however, Freddie overwhelmed me with his faith and I found myself committed to the duty of commending the proposal to the Management Committee of the Outward Bound Trust. They responded in ritualistic fashion. I was made Chairman of a sub-committee to investigate the feasibility of the whole idea and make recommendations!

Pressed for details Freddie Fuller left us in no doubt that here was something with real potential. The need was for collaborators who commanded the necessary physical resources in an urban setting. We were fortunate in that our first approach was to the Education Authority of the City of Leeds. Offers of collaboration included the use of the Carnegie College of Physical Education with its residential accommodation, gymnasia, swimming bath and specialist staff.

As a result, in July, 1967, "City Challenge," the first Outward Bound course in an urban situation, was run jointly with the Leeds Education Committee under Freddie Fuller's general direction.

The boys undertook an exciting programme of physical education which included drown-proofing, canoe rolling, trampolining, and judo. Small groups in turn manned the casualty reception points of local hospitals, worked in a hostel for down-and-outs, assisted with play groups largely composed of immigrant children, and restored order in the homes of people who had rejected all the normal services. Finally they created a splendid adventure playground on waste land in a new housing estate. Those who took part and those who saw the course seem unanimous in the belief that this is a form of training which must be continued. There will be further experimental courses and it is hoped that, as a result, an entirely new field of development will have opened up in which a private organisation may combine with a series of public authorities to fill a gap in the social services and at the same time afford an opportunity to young people to grow in responsibility and understanding.

CHAPTER 19

It would be fitting to conclude with some reflections on the indirect consequences of Hahn's original inspiration. There can surely be no doubt that the growth of centres for "adventure training" and the increased interest in various "outdoor pursuits" have taken their stimulus very largely from the success of the Outward Bound Schools. Similarly it would not be difficult to trace a connection between Hahn's efforts to generalise the Moray Badge—first through the County Badge Experimental Committee and later through the practices of the Outward Bound Schools — and the Duke of Edinburgh's Award Scheme. As a result of all these endeavours large numbers of people—young and old—are now pursuing sports and pastimes previously enjoyed only by a few. Climbing, caving, canoeing, sailing, ski-ing, underwater swimming — all command their devotees in increasing numbers and from a widening cross-section of the community. All have in common one characteristic — the price of carelessness can be severe indeed. And in nearly all cases carelessness by any one participant can result in the involvement of rescue teams — many of them voluntary — who may be called upon to expose themselves to considerable risk.

It is ironic that an increasing toll of accidents in the mountains and on the water should be in any way traceable to Hahn's initial impulse. One of the most remarkable things about this remarkable man is the strain he constantly suffers because of the risks involved in the enterprises he has launched. Whenever one of our ships ran into any kind of difficulty Hahn would go through a nightmare of anxiety and, once the episode was over, would insist on most careful investigation in order to avoid the possibility of a repetition.

It was because of this that patterns of practice were developed in Outward Bound Schools which enabled them to operate for nearly twenty years without a fatal accident. When one described the activities of the schools to audiences of laymen it was commonplace for someone to ask, "How many have you killed?" From time to time I remember parties of officers responsible for the training of Commandos or Marines visiting the school to discover why it was that, reputedly, we were submitting boys to exercises frequently as hazardous as those used in advanced military training yet without casualties. The answer was, I think, fairly simple. In wartime training commanders often put men into situations in order that they may be stretched in initiative and enterprise in extricating themselves from trouble. Thanks to Hahn, however, our teaching was that a man should never expose himself to hazard until he had made a thorough assessment of the risks involved and, as fully as possible, safeguarded himself against them. It was not uncommon to meet men engaged in military training whose watchword was "We make 'em or break 'em." Our task was clearly to make rather than break. Boys gained in confidence and competence as they went through graded exercises. We taught that bravado and recklessness were no substitute for skill and foresight and that as far as we were concerned they were completely taboo.

Thus it was that for close on twenty years one could boast a fatality-free record. As in that time something approaching 40,000 youngsters must have passed through the schools this was no mean boast. Had they been going about their normal occasions on the streets of this country instead of engaging in strenuous exercises on the sea and the mountains it would not have been unreasonable to expect that the casualty rate might have been higher. It was the recognition of this fact that led one to conclude that we had been protected not only by our own care and prudence but also by a large element of luck. There had, of course, been occasional incidents when some foolish or feckless youth had ignored all the precepts and principles of our training but had been saved from anything worse than a wetting or a bad bruising by the intervention of Providence. One was fully aware that this could not go on for ever but heartily grateful that our good fortune held as long as it did. A fatal accident in the early days would have proved a severe setback. Even if it were to be clear that the school was completely free of negligence, critics would undoubtedly have argued that there was something inherently foolhardy in the whole conception.

It was at Eskdale that eventually the run was broken. An expedition party accompanied by an instructor was returning to the school by one of the higher routes after a wet night on the fells. The conditions were unpleasant but by no means extreme; the party appeared to be in cheerful spirits and good shape. Accordingly, as was common practice, the instructor deemed that he could safely leave the patrol to complete the journey unaccompanied. Shortly after he had left, one of the boys began to exhibit the symptoms about which we now know a great deal — the symptoms of exposure. Training for such an eventuality has now reached a very high peak of efficiency and everyone has been put very much on guard. Though at that time less emphasis had been placed upon the symptoms and treatment of exposure the boys acted with great good sense. When they realised that efforts to get the boy down to the lower levels were doomed to failure they gave him all the protection they could and despatched runners for help. By the time a rescue party arrived this boy was dead and all efforts to revive him were fruitless.

At the inquest it was revealed that the boy had an unusual sensitivity to cold. The school had been unaware of this, nor had this weakness previously manifested itself during the course. Expert medical evidence was called and the verdict totally exonerated the school of any lack of care or responsibility. Nevertheless the Trust, very properly, set up an expert committee of enquiry to consider every aspect of what had occurred so as to ensure that in future even the exceptionally vulnerable might be protected. Every detail of the equipment used for camping on the previous night, of the food consumed and of the clothing used was subjected to rigorous examination. The school immediately obtained such revised clothing and equipment as seemed likely to contribute to greater safety and the first aid training was revised so as to emphasise the treatment of exposure.

From this time forward all of the schools which made use of the mountains began to devote a great deal of thought to the special hazards presented by bad weather.

Needless to say there is no chance of arriving at total guarantees in this matter. If, as appears probable, training in responsibility can best be carried out when the price of irresponsibility is clear, then there will be a case for continuing to expose the young to situations fraught with some minimum of reasonable risk. One could argue that the Outward Bound record in this country is not such as to occasion alarm. Those responsible however are not content to take comfort in statistics. The Trust has set up a permanent Safety Committee composed of people whose experience on the sea and the mountains is widely recognised as highly authoritative. They have laid down a code of practice which simply must be observed in all the schools. What is more, they must be informed of all mishaps — including "near-misses" — so that the whole situation may be kept under constant review.

One might be forgiven for feeling much less anxiety about what happens in Outward Bound schools than about the effects of more widespread adoption of adventurous outdoor pursuits for which the success of Outward Bound must in some measure be responsible. It is good that more and more young people are being introduced to the sea and the mountains for healthy recreation, but many of the well-meaning adults who lead them in such pursuits are insufficiently aware of the dangers involved and the technical training that is essential to safety. Constantly in the mountains one meets parties which are ill-shod, inadequately clothed and obviously ignorant of the rigours with which they could be faced by a sudden change of weather. The rising toll of holiday and week-end accidents is now stirring a proper concern about these things. The first steps have been taken to establish a recognised training for mountain leadership and the Central Council for Physical Recreation has already done much to establish good standards for most of the adventurous recreations. It is to be hoped that all who feel disposed to open up to succeeding generations the healthy heritage of our seas and mountains will give their support and encouragement to these developments.

One of Hahn's most memorable statements was:

"It is wrong to coerce people into opinions, but it is a duty to impel them into experiences."

To those who seek to adopt Hahn's precept one would like to stress that behind all his practices there was a passionate concern that youngsters should not merely survive the experiences into which he plunged them but that they should emerge strengthened. If Outward Bound has demonstrated anything it must surely be that adventure should be used as an ingredient in education only by those who have accepted the restraints and disciplines which are essential to successful practice.